Step Language for Everyday Life
Forward

Workbook

SERIES DIRECTOR
Jayme Adelson-Goldstein

1

Janet Podnecky

OXFORD
UNIVERSITY PRESS

OXFORD
UNIVERSITY PRESS

198 Madison Avenue
New York, NY 10016 USA

Great Clarendon Street, Oxford OX2 6DP UK

Oxford University Press is a department of the University of Oxford.
It furthers the University's objective of excellence in research, scholarship,
and education by publishing worldwide in

Oxford New York

Auckland Cape Town Dar es Salaam Hong Kong Karachi
Kuala Lumpur Madrid Melbourne Mexico City Nairobi
New Delhi Shanghai Taipei Toronto

With offices in

Argentina Austria Brazil Chile Czech Republic France Greece
Guatemala Hungary Italy Japan Poland Portugal Singapore
South Korea Switzerland Thailand Turkey Ukraine Vietnam

OXFORD and OXFORD ENGLISH are registered trademarks of
Oxford University Press

Executive Publisher: Janet Aitchison
Editorial Manager: Stephanie Karras
Associate Editor: Ashli Caudle Totty
Art Director: Maj-Britt Hagsted
Senior Art Editor: Judi DeSouter
Production Manager: Shanta Persaud
Production Controller: Robin Roberson

ISBN: 978 0 19 4392327

Printed in Hong Kong
10 9 8 7 6 5 4

Illustrations: Susan Spellman: pp. 2, 5, 11, 16, 24, 39, 57, 61, 65; Richard
Deverell: pp. 6, 18, 31, 33, 51, 55, 73; Kevin Brown: pp. 25, 40, 47, 52, 59,
63, 74, 76, 84; Kathy Baxendale: pp. 2, 9, 23, 30, 41, 44, 72, 78, 79; Gary
Torrisi: 7, 13, 26, 37, 46, 58, 68, 82; Karen Minot: pp. 20, 34, 44, 45, 80.

Photographs: Inmagine: Photodisc, 4, 38, 65; Stockbyte, 19; Brand X
Pictures, 19; Banana Stock, 23, 53; Stockdisc, 56; Alamy: Blend Images,
10; Jupiter Images: Photos.com, 17, 23; Able Stock, 14 ; Index Open:
Photolibrary.com, 17; Fogstock LLC, 83; Photo Edit Inc.: Eric Fowke, 28;
Felicia Martinez, 56; Jeff Greenberg, 65; Dana White, 66; Bill Aron, 70;
Michael Newman, 77; Index Stock: Lauree Feldman,, 32; David Collado –
FDNY, 35; Masterfile: Scott Tysick, 65; Masterfile RF, 42, 81; Dreamstime.
com: Mehmet Alci, 67; Harry Cutting Photography, 16.

I would like to express my deep gratitude to Ashli Totty
for her encouragement and patience throughout this
project. I am also grateful to Meg Brooks and others
on the team at Oxford University Press who offered so
many ideas and suggestions.

I'm especially thankful to my family, Josef and Michelle,
for their support and understanding when the midnight
oil had to be burned.

Janet Podnecky

It's been a privilege to work with Step Forward's gifted
team of editors, designers, and authors. Special thanks
to Janet Podnecky—for her ability to go beyond "fill in
the blank," to Ashli Totty—for her expertise and good
humor, to Meg Brooks—for her point of view, and to
Jane Spigarelli—for the book without which this book
would not be.

For those who love the phrase "Open your workbook."

Jayme Adelson-Goldstein

CONTENTS

A Look at the pictures. Match the words with the pictures.

_____ say   _____ open   _____ close   _____ repeat

_1_ listen to   _____ point to   _____ sit down   _____ stand up

B Read the words. Look around the classroom. Circle the singular and plural words for the things and people you see.

1. a chair / chairs
2. a teacher / teachers
3. a student / students
4. a desk / desks
5. a book / books
6. a pen / pens
7. a clock / clocks
8. a board / boards

A Read the form.

School Registration Form

Name: _____Martinez_____Elena_____
                    (last)   (first)

Address: __118 Linden Street, Apt. 18, Andover, MA 21156__
                      (street)   (city/state)   (zip code)

Telephone: __(617) 555-1345_____
                     (area code)

Email: __emartinez@work.us_____

Signature: ____Elena Martinez_____

B Look at the form in A. Circle *a* or *b*.

1. Tell me your first name.
   a. Martinez
   (b.) Elena
2. Tell me your telephone number.
   a. (617) 555-1345
   b. 21156
3. Write your email address.
   a. emartinez@work.us
   b. 118 Linden Street

4. Please spell your last name.
   a. M-A-R-T-I-N-E-Z
   b. E-L-E-N-A
5. Please write your address.
   a. Elena Martinez
   b. 118 Linden Street, Apt. 18
6. Please sign your name.
   a. Elena Martinez
   b. Elena Martinez

C Complete the form. Use your own information. Sign your name.

School Registration Form

Name: _____
                    (last)   (first)

Address: _____
                      (street)   (city/state)   (zip code)

Telephone: _____
                     (area code)

Email: _____

Signature: _____

LESSON 3   Grammar

A Circle the correct words.

1. He (**is** / are) a student.

2. We (are / is) in class.

3. I (am / is) not a teacher.

4. They (is / are) my classmates.

5. You (are / am) in my group.

6. It (am / is) my book.

7. Mr. Sims (is / are) my teacher.

8. She (is / are) my friend.

B Complete the sentences. Use *am, is,* or *are.*

1. He _____is_____ my partner.

2. We _____ in the classroom.

3. You _____ a teacher.

4. They _____ in my group.

5. I _____ at my desk.

6. It _____ my dictionary.

7. She _____ a student.

8. Elena and Dan _____ teachers.

C Rewrite the sentences in B. Make them negative.

1. He is not my partner.

2. _____

3. _____

4. _____

5. _____

6. _____

7. _____

8. _____

D Rewrite the sentences. Use contractions for the underlined words.

1. <u>I am</u> a student.　　　　I'm a student.

2. We <u>are not</u> teachers.　　_____

3. The teacher <u>is not</u> here.　_____

4. She <u>is not</u> in the classroom.　_____

5. <u>You are</u> my partner.　　_____

6. <u>They are</u> listening.　　_____

7. <u>I am</u> not at school.　　_____

8. <u>He is</u> a teacher.　　　_____

E ✎ **Grammar Boost**　Unscramble the sentences.

1. am / in / not / I / the classroom

   I am not in the classroom.

2. not / students / They / are

   _____

3. classmate / You / my / are

   _____

4. We / in / school / are

   _____

5. my / is / It / book

   _____

6. teacher / not / is / She / my

   _____

A Complete the conversation. Use the words in the box.

you later	And you	~~Good morning~~	Fine	How are

Ana: Good morning, Mr. Han.

Mr. Han: _Good morning_ , Ana.
                        1

Ana: _____ you?
                        2

Mr. Han: Fine, thanks. _____?
                                    3

Ana: _____. See _____, Mr. Han.
                        4   5

Mr. Han: Goodbye, Ana.

B Complete the conversation. Use your own information.

1. **A:** Hi, I'm Nadel. What's your name?

   B: _____

2. **A:** Can you repeat that, please?

   B: _____

3. **A:** How are you?

   B: _____

4. **A:** It's nice to meet you.

   B: _____

5. **A:** Goodbye.

   B: _____

LESSON 5 Real-life reading

A Look at the pictures. Write the correct words under each picture. Use the words in the box.

~~study~~ go to school listen to the radio ask for help

1. _____study_____   2. _____   3. _____   4. _____

B Look at the chart. Match the numbers with the information.

How Students in Class 2B Study English

Study Methods	Number of Adults
speak English at home	6
read in English	4
listen to the radio	12 +
study at home	3

How many students...

_d_ 1. read in English?   a. 3 students

____ 2. study at home?   b. 6 students

____ 3. listen to the radio?   c. 12+ students

____ 4. speak English at home?   d. 4 students

C How do you learn English? Check (✔) your study method.

____ read in English   ____ listen to the radio

____ study at home   ____ speak English at home

A Complete the questions and the instructions. Use the code.

1=a	2=b	3=c	4=d	5=e	6=f
7=g	8=h	9=i	10=j	11=k	12=l
13=m	14=n	15=o	16=p	17=q	18=r
19=s	20=t	21=u	22=v	23=w	24=x
25=y	26=z				

1. W h a t ' s your f i r s t n a m e ?
   23 8 1 20 19 6 9 18 19 20 14 1 13 5

2. How a r e _____ ?
   1 18 5 25 15 21

3. _____ _____ your _____.
   20 5 12 12 13 5 1 4 4 18 5 19 19

4. _____ , _____ _____ number?
   23 8 1 20 19 25 15 21 18 16 8 15 14 5

5. _____ your _____.
   19 9 7 14 14 1 13 5

B Look at A. Answer the questions and follow the instructions. Use complete sentences and your own information.

What's your first name? My first name is...

1. _____
2. _____
3. _____
4. _____
5. _____

UNIT 2

My Classmates

LESSON 1 **Vocabulary**

A Look at the clocks. Write the times two ways.

1. _5:00_____

   _five o'clock_____

2. _____

   _____

3. _____

   _____

4. _____

   _____

5. _____

   _____

6. _____

   _____

B Complete the chart. Use the words in the box.

| ~~Monday~~ | 11/20/88 | Friday | ~~5:45~~ | 4:30 | March |
| October | January | 3/16/05 | 7/18/07 | Thursday | 2:00 |

Time	Day	Month	Date
5:45	Monday		

A Read the form.

Personal Information Form

Name: _Valdez_ _Gina_
(last) (first)

Address: _231 River Avenue, Apt. 9A_
(street)

Miami, FL 74354
(city/state) (zip code)

Telephone: _(918) 555-6721_
(area code)

Place of Birth: _El Salvador_

Florida DRIVER'S LICENSE

ID# 4882193929

Date of Birth:
06-30-1977

EXP. DATE:
06-30-2007

Gina Valdez

Gina Valdez
231 River Avenue, Apt. 9A
Miami, FL 74354

DL

B Look at the form in A. Complete the sentences.

1. My _____name_____ is Gina Valdez.

2. I'm from _____.

3. My _____ of birth is June 30, 1977.

4. My _____ number is (918) 555-6721.

5. I _____ in Miami, FL.

6. My _____ is 231 River Avenue, Apt. 9A.

C Answer the questions. Use complete sentences and your own information.

1. What's your name?

   _____

2. Where are you from?

   _____

3. What's your date of birth?

   _____

4. Where do you live?

   _____

5. What's your address?

   _____

6. What's your telephone number?

   _____

A Look at the pictures. Write the correct words under the pictures. Use the words in the box.

| tired   happy   angry   ~~worried~~   hungry   proud |

1. _____worried_____   3. _____   5. _____

2. _____   4. _____   6. _____

B Match the questions with the answers.

_c_ 1. Are you angry?   a. Yes, they are.

___ 2. Is Paul tired?   b. No, we're not.

___ 3. Is Sophie worried?   c. No, I'm not.

___ 4. Are the students happy?   d. Yes, he is.

___ 5. Are you and Paul hungry?   e. No, she isn't.

C Read the sentences. Then write *Yes/No* questions. Use the words in parentheses.

1. Sara is from New York. (Mark)

   Is Mark from New York? _____

2. Nadel and Tom are proud. (Lilia)

   _____

3. Anh is from Vietnam. (Carol and Pam)

   _____

4. We are tired. (Daniel)

   _____

5. I am hungry. (you)

   _____

D Read the answers. Write the *Yes/No* questions. Use the words in parentheses.

1. (you / sad)

   A: Are you sad?

   B: Yes, I am.

2. (the students / tired)

   A: _____

   B: No, they aren't.

3. (Juan / from Mexico)

   A: _____

   B: No, he isn't.

4. (the teacher / in the classroom)

   A: _____

   B: Yes, she is.

5. (this workbook / yellow)

   A: _____

   B: Yes, it is.

6. (we / studying)

   A: _____

   B: No, we aren't.

E 🚀 **Grammar Boost** Unscramble the questions. Then match the questions with the answers.

_c_ 1. name / your / What / is

     What is your name?

____ 2. from / you / Where / are

     _____

____ 3. your / What / is / date of birth

     _____

____ 4. is / Where / Luc

     _____

a. I'm from Haiti.
b. He's in the classroom.
c. My name is Eric.
d. My date of birth is 6/10/85.

LESSON 4 Everyday conversation

A Read the form.

Personal Information Form

Name: ___Peng_____Yoshi_____
              (last)   (first)

Address: ___3933 Ross Avenue, San Jose, CA 95124___
             (street)   (city/state)   (zip code)

Telephone: ___(209) 555-7455_____
           (area code)

Date of Birth: ___5/6/76___

Place of Birth: ___Japan___

Marital Status: (married)   single

B Look at the form in A. Answer the questions. Use complete sentences.

1. What's your last name?

   My last name is Peng.

2. What's your first name?

   _____

3. Are you married or single?

   _____

4. What's your address?

   _____

5. What's your date of birth?

   _____

6. Where are you from?

   _____

C Answer the questions. Use your own information.

1. What's your last name?

   _____

2. Are you married or single?

   _____

3. Where are you from?

   _____

4. What's your date of birth?

   _____

A Complete the sentences. Use the words in the box.

> population   countries   ~~million~~

1. 1,000,000 is one ____million____.

2. China and India are _____ in Asia.

3. The _____ of the United States is 295 million people.

B Read the article.

California: An Interesting State

California is a state in the United States. Today, the population of California is about 36 million people. 11.6 million are Latin American. 3.9 million are Asian. Nine million are from other countries. Six million are students.

C Look at the article in B. Circle *a* or *b*.

1. California is a ____.
   (a.) state
   b. country

2. What is the population of California?
   a. 36 million people
   b. 3.9 million people

3. Are 11.6 million Latin Americans in California?
   a. Yes
   b. No

4. Are nine million students in California?
   a. Yes
   b. No

UNIT 2   Another look

A Look at the chart. Cross out (X) the example word that does not belong in each line.

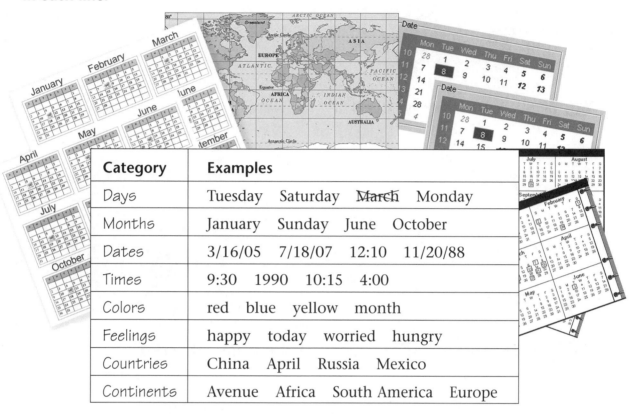

Category	Examples
Days	Tuesday Saturday ~~March~~ Monday
Months	January Sunday June October
Dates	3/16/05 7/18/07 12:10 11/20/88
Times	9:30 1990 10:15 4:00
Colors	red blue yellow month
Feelings	happy today worried hungry
Countries	China April Russia Mexico
Continents	Avenue Africa South America Europe

B Write sentences. Use a word from each category.

(Day) <u>Today is Wednesday.</u>   (Continent) <u>Sam is from Africa.</u>

1. (Days) _____

2. (Months) _____

3. (Dates) _____

4. (Times) _____

5. (Colors) _____

6. (Feelings) _____

7. (Countries) _____

8. (Continents) _____

UNIT 3

Family and Friends

LESSON 1 Vocabulary

A Who is in your family? Check (✔) the words.

_____ husband   _____ brother

_____ wife   _____ sister

_____ father   _____ aunt

_____ mother   _____ uncle

_____ son   _____ grandfather

_____ daughter   _____ grandmother

_____ children   _____ cousin

B Look at Christine and her family. Complete the sentences.

Grandparents

John   Amy

Father   Mother

Joe   Sarin

Brother

Al   Christine

1. Sarin is the ____mother____.

2. _____ is the brother.

3. Joe is the _____.

4. John and _____ are the _____.

16   Unit 3 Lesson 1

A Look at the ID cards. Complete the sentences.

My _____name_____ is Marie.
      1

_____ _____ are brown.
     2   3

My _____ _____ black.
      4   5

DMV **CALIFORNIA** DMV
IDENTIFICATION CARD

Marie Santos
ID# 673-9295011

Eye Color: brown

Hair Color: black

Marie Santos

My name is _____.
                 6

My eyes _____ _____.
              7   8

_____ _____ is blond.
     9   10

DMV **CALIFORNIA** DMV
IDENTIFICATION CARD

Pavel Turek
ID# 842-1314772

Eye Color: blue

Hair Color: blond

Pavel Turek

B Answer the questions. Use complete sentences and your own information.

What is your name? My name is David.

1. What is your name?

   _____

2. What color are your eyes?

   _____

3. What color is your hair?

   _____

4. Are you tall or short?

   _____

5. Are you heavy, average, or thin?

   _____

6. Are you young?

   _____

A Circle the correct words.

1. Hi. (My / Your) name is Ines.

2. This is Ron. (Their / His) brother is in this class.

3. We are in the class. (Her / Our) teacher is Mr. Flynn.

4. Rita is in class. (Her / His) papers are on the table.

5. Where are the students? (Their / Her) books are here.

6. This is for you. It's (their / your) book.

B Match the questions with the answers.

  _d_   1. Is your sister tall?   a. Yes, they are brown.

_____ 2. Are your eyes blue?   b. Yes, she is here.

_____ 3. Is Mark's hair blond?   c. Yes, I'm their friend.

_____ 4. Are Karen's eyes brown?   d. Yes, she is tall.

_____ 5. Is my sister in class today?   e. No, his hair is brown.

_____ 6. Are you Sam and Tom's friend?   f. No, my eyes are green.

C Complete the sentences. Use possessive adjectives that match the underlined words.

1. I like _____my_____ family and friends.

2. Sasha is a good friend. She has a big family. _____ family is nice.

3. Olga is in school. _____ family is from Russia.

4. David and Tony are not in this class, but _____ sister is.

5. We like the class and _____ teacher.

6. Are you a new student? What's _____ name?

7. The school is good. _____ name is South Street Training Center.

8. Are you and Paul ready? Where are _____ books?

D Look at the ID cards. Write 3 sentences about each person. Use possessive adjectives and the words in parentheses.

CALIFORNIA
DMV DMV
IDENTIFICATION CARD

Paul Allen
ID# 973-9265021
Eye Color: blue
Hair Color: black

Paul Allen

1. (name) <u>His name is Paul Allen.</u>
2. (eyes) _____
3. (hair) _____

CALIFORNIA
DMV DMV
IDENTIFICATION CARD

Sasha Tomlin
ID# 879-6318794
Eye Color: green
Hair Color: blond

Sasha Tomlin

4. (name) _____
5. (eyes) _____
6. (hair) _____

E 🚀 **Grammar Boost** Complete the questions with *Paul's* or *Sasha's*. Then complete the answers with *his* or *her*.

1. **A:** What is <u>Paul's</u> last name?

   B: <u>His</u> last name is Allen.

2. **A:** What color are _____ eyes?

   B: _____ eyes are blue.

3. **A:** What is _____ last name?

   B: _____ last name is Tomlin.

4. **A:** What color is _____ hair?

   B: _____ hair is blond.

5. **A:** What color is _____ hair?

   B: _____ hair is black.

6. **A:** What is _____ ID #?

   B: _____ ID# is 879-6318794.

7. **A:** What color are _____ eyes?

   B: _____ eyes are green.

8. **A:** What is _____ ID #?

   B: _____ ID# is 973-9265021.

A Complete the conversation. Use the words in the box.

the date today	~~day is today~~	birthday
October 10th	that's right	It's Tuesday

David: Hi, Marie. What _day is today_____?

                                 1

Marie: _____.

                        2

David: What's _____?

                        3

Marie: It's _____.

                       4

David: Tuesday, October 10th?

Marie: Yes, _____.

                       5

David: Oh, no. Today is Tom's _____.

                       6

B Write the dates.

1. 3/16 _March 16th_   3. 2/22 _____   5. 11/20 _____

2. 6/21 _____   4. 8/9 _____   6. 7/31 _____

C Look at the calendar. Answer the questions. Use complete sentences.

1. What day is today? _Today is Friday._____

2. What is the date? _____

3. When is Marie's birthday? _____

4. What day is June 9th? _____

A Look at the graph. Read the article.

Families in the United States

In the United States, families are large and small. There are families with many children. There are families with no children. In many families, there is a married couple at home. In other families, there is only an adult male[1] at home.

In other families, there is only an adult female[2] at home.

[1]male = man
[2]female = woman

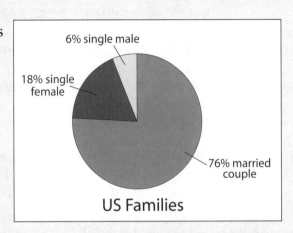

6% single male

18% single female

76% married couple

US Families

B Look at the article and graph in A. Circle *a* or *b*.

1. In the United States, families are large and _____.
   a. married
   b. small

2. In eighteen percent of families, there is _____.
   a. only an adult woman
   b. only an adult male

3. In seventy-six percent of families, there is _____.
   a. many children
   b. a married couple

4. In _____ of families, there is only an adult man at home.
   a. eighteen percent
   b. six percent

A Unscramble the words.

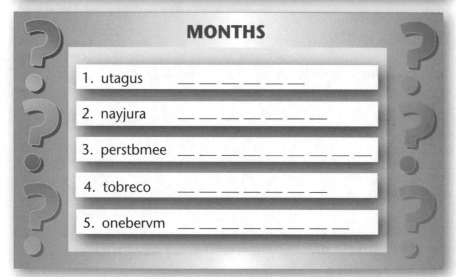

DAYS

1. dasnuy   S u n d a y
2. rfdyai   _ _ _ _ _ _
3. styurhad   _ _ _ _ _ _ _ _
4. staudey   _ _ _ _ _ _ _
5. edewndsya   _ _ _ _ _ _ _ _ _

MONTHS

1. utagus   _ _ _ _ _ _
2. nayjura   _ _ _ _ _ _ _
3. perstbmee   _ _ _ _ _ _ _ _ _
4. tobreco   _ _ _ _ _ _ _
5. onebervm   _ _ _ _ _ _ _ _

B Complete the words in each sentence with one letter. Use the letters in the box.

| a | e | i | o | u |

1. Th_i_s _i_s my s_i_ster Sue.
2. Sue's h___ir is bl___ck.
3. H___r ___y___s ar___ gr___ ___n.
4. My ___unt is t___ll ___nd be___utiful.
5. O___r ___ncle has bl___e eyes.
6. Y___ur c___usin's hair is br___wn.

UNIT 4

At Home

LESSON 1 **Vocabulary**

A **Match the words with the pictures.**

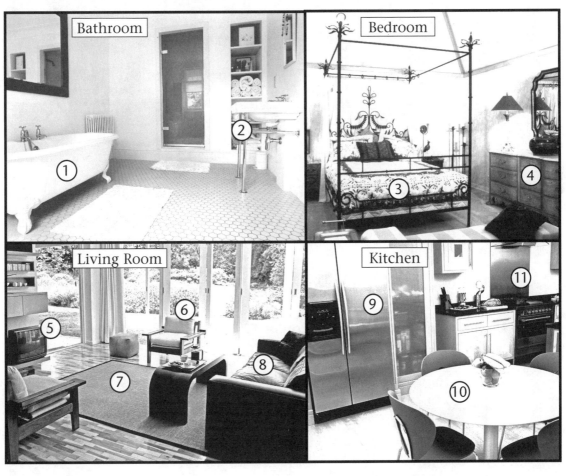

____ bed	____ sofa	____ refrigerator	____ TV
____ table	_1_ bathtub	____ stove	____ rug
____ sink	____ dresser	____ chair	

B **Look at the pictures in A. Answer the questions. Use complete sentences.**

1. Where's the sofa? <u>The sofa is in the living room.</u>

2. Where's the stove? _____

3. Is the bed in the kitchen? _____

4. Is the sofa in the bedroom? _____

A **Look at the picture. Complete the sentences. Use the words in the box.**

living room	washing the car	~~listening to music~~	yard
the kitchen	playing games	cooking dinner	bedroom

It's a beautiful day. Mrs. Vegas is _____listening to music_____. She's in the

_____. Mr. Vegas is in _____. He's
      2   3

_____. Clara is sleeping. She's in the _____.
      4   5

David and Linda are _____ in the _____. Luis
            6   7

is outside. He's _____. It's a great day to do some work or relax.
          8

B **Mrs. Vegas is talking about her house. Complete the sentences with**
This, That, These, **or** *Those***.**

This/These

1. __This_____ is our house.

2. _____ is our yard.
   It's small, but nice.

3. _____ flowers are pretty
   right now.

That/Those

1. _____ is my daughter.

2. _____ is my daughter's
   friend, David.

3. _____ are their school
   books.

A **Circle the correct words.**

1. Hi. My name is Ellen. ((I)/ He) am cleaning the kitchen.

2. This is my roommate, Claire. (She / We) is studying.

3. (We / I) are cooking dinner.

4. (He / You) are eating with us tonight, right?

5. These are our friends. (He / They) are playing in the yard.

6. Now, (you / I) am dusting the table.

B **Complete the sentences. Use the present continuous and the verbs in parentheses.**

1. We _____are watching_____ a video right now. (watch)

2. Our teacher _____ some work. (do)

3. I _____ the newspaper. (read)

4. Javier and Eduardo _____ in the kitchen. (eat)

5. Patty _____ in the bedroom. (sleep)

6. The teacher _____ to her. (listen)

C **Write sentences. Use the present continuous.**

1. We / clean / the house / today
   We are cleaning the house today.

2. My / brother / mop / the kitchen
   _____

3. Our / friends / wash / the car
   _____

4. My / mother / vacuum / the rug
   _____

5. Our / cousin / dust / the bookcase
   _____

6. I / watch / TV
   _____

D Look at the pictures. Write information questions. Then write the answers. Use the present continuous.

Laura

1. What is Laura doing?
   She's studying.

Patty and Rose

2. _____
   _____

David and Maritza

3. _____
   _____

Pete

4. _____
   _____

E **Grammar Boost** Add *-ing.* Rewrite the verbs.

1. play → playing
2. mop → _____
3. do → _____
4. give → _____
5. close → _____
6. stop → _____

A **Read the bills.**

Central State Electric Co.	**CellTele Phone Co.**	**Hydro-Clear**
Amount due: $52.50	Amount due: $88.00	*Amount due:* $25.00
due date 5/12/08	due date 5/23/08	due date 5/27/08

B **Complete the conversation. Use words in the box.**

May 12th	the electric bill	~~are you~~
I help you	the due date	paying

Minh: What _____ are you _____ doing?
1

John: I'm _____ the bills.
2

Minh: Can _____?
3

John: Yes, please. Where's _____?
4

Minh: Here it is.

John: What's _____?
5

Minh: It's _____.
6

John: Oh, that's tomorrow! I'm paying that bill today!

C **Rewrite the sentences. Use the pronouns in the chart for the underlined words.**

1. <u>Bob</u> is paying <u>the bills</u>.

   He is paying them.

2. <u>Minh and Bob</u> are looking at <u>the calendar</u>.

   _____

3. <u>Minh and I</u> are calling <u>Bob</u>.

   _____

4. I'm giving <u>the games</u> to <u>Rose</u>.

   _____

5. <u>Rose</u> is listening to <u>the radio</u>.

   _____

6. <u>The company</u> is sending the bill to <u>my brother and me</u>.

   _____

Grammar note

Subject pronouns	Object pronouns
I	me
you	you
he	him
she	her
it	it
we	us
they	them

A Read the tips.

More Tips To Save Money

1. Look at the bills. Check the dates.

2. Talk to your family. Say, "Turn off the lights."

3. Take five-minute showers.

4. Ask friends, "Is there a different phone company or gas company?"

5. Call the companies. Ask, "What are your prices?"

6. Write down their answers and ideas.

7. Next month, check the new bills. Are you saving some money?

B Read the sentences. Check (✔) the ideas in the article. Mark (X) the ideas NOT in the article.

___✓___ 1. These tips help you save money.

_____ 2. Check the dates on the bills.

_____ 3. Your family helps save on the utilities.

_____ 4. All companies have the same prices.

_____ 5. Ask friends about different companies.

_____ 6. Don't call long distance.

A Complete the sentences. Use the words in the box.

mopping	~~bills~~	phone	paying	electric
eating	bedroom	cleaning	stove	

1. I pay the utility ___bills___ every month.

2. It's Saturday. We're _____ all the rooms in the house.

3. Paul is cooking on the _____ in the kitchen.

4. Please pay the telephone, gas, water, and _____ bills tomorrow.

5. I am _____ the floor.

6. Kara is sleeping in the _____.

7. I'm talking on the _____.

8. We are _____ dinner at 6:00.

9. Are you _____ the bills today?

B Complete the puzzle. Use the words in A.

1. b i l l (s)
2. __ __ __ (O) __ __ __ __
3. __ __ __ (O) __
4. __ __ (O) __ __ __ __
5. (O) __ __ __ __ __
6. __ __ __ __ (O) __ __
7. __ __ __ (O) __
8. (O) __ __ __ __
9. __ __ (O) __ __ __

C Write the circled letters from the puzzle in B. What's the secret message?

___ ___ ___ ___   ___ ___ ___ ___ ___ !
 1   2   3   4   5   6   7   8   9

UNIT 5

In the Neighborhood

LESSON 1 **Vocabulary**

A Look at the map. Match the words with the picture.

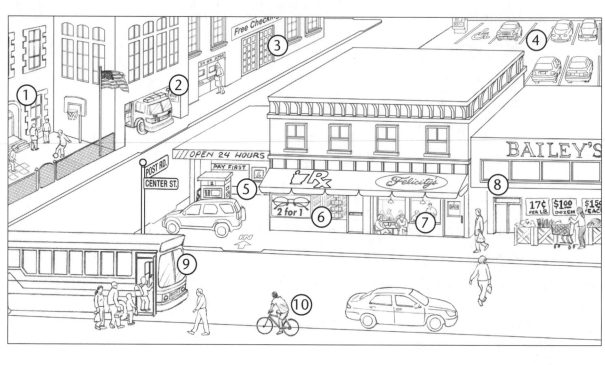

____ supermarket   ____ fire station   ____ bicycle   ____ bus stop   ____ bank

_1_ school   ____ restaurant   ____ gas station   ____ pharmacy   ____ parking lot

B Look at the map. Answer the questions. Use complete sentences.

1. Where is the bank?

   The bank is on Post Road.

2. Where is the fire station?

   _____

3. Where is the supermarket?

   _____

4. Where is the school?

   _____

A **Look at the picture. Match the places with the locations.**

_b_ 1. The apartment building is   a. across from the apartment building.

____ 2. The bank is   b. next to the bank.

____ 3. The post office is   c. between the supermarket and the apartment building.

____ 4. The pharmacy is   d. across from the bank.

B **Look at the picture in A. Complete the sentences. Use the words in the box.**

my neighborhood	an apartment	next to the
a bank	across from my	~~I live~~

1. _I live_____ on River Street. It's a nice place to live.

2. I live in _____ there. The address is 2919 River Street.

3. In _____, there are many places.

4. There is a post office _____ apartment building.

5. There is a pharmacy _____ post office.

6. There is _____ between my apartment and the supermarket.

A Complete the sentences. Use *There is* or *There are*.

Southside Mall is a great place for shoppers!

1. _There are_ _____ over 50 stores in the mall.
2. _____ three banks in the mall.
3. _____ a large parking lot.
4. _____ two movie theaters.
5. _____ eight restaurants.
6. _____ not a post office.
7. _____ not a supermarket.
8. _____ two pharmacies.

B Write sentences. Use *There is* and *There are*.

1. There / many places / in / my neighborhood

   There are many places in my neighborhood. _____

2. There / a movie theater / across from / my home

   _____

3. There / some restaurants / next to / the school

   _____

4. There / a parking lot / behind / the school

   _____

5. There / an apartment building / between / the school / and / the park

   _____

6. There / a bus stop / in front of / the movie theater

   _____

7. There / a supermarket / next to / the park

   _____

8. There / a hospital / behind / the supermarket

   _____

C Look at the picture. Complete the questions. Use *Is there* or *Are there*. Then answer the questions.

1. **A:** <u>Is there</u> a boy on a bicycle?

   B: <u>Yes, there is.</u>

2. **A:** _____ a dog in the park?

   B: _____

3. **A:** _____ a man with a computer?

   B: _____

4. **A:** _____ restaurants in the park?

   B: _____

5. **A:** _____ children in the park?

   B: _____

6. **A:** _____ a bus stop near the park?

   B: _____

D 🚀 **Grammar Boost** Write about your neighborhood. Complete the questions. Use *Is there* or *Are there*. Then write your answers. If you say *yes*, give the location.

Is there a library in your neighborhood?
Yes, there is. It's next to the pharmacy.

1. A: _____ a library in your neighborhood?

   B: _____

2. A: _____ a fire station?

   B: _____

3. A: _____ restaurants?

   B: _____

4. A: _____ banks?

   B: _____

LESSON 4 Everyday conversation

A Look at the map. Complete the conversation. Use the words in the box.

~~Excuse~~   there   straight   left   blocks   turn   right   between

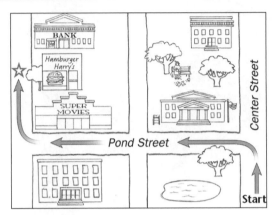

A: <u>Excuse</u> me. Is _____ a restaurant near here?
     1   2

B: Yes, there is. Go _____ on Center Street. Turn _____ on Pond
                           3   4

Street. Go two _____ on Pond Street. Then, _____ right.
                   5   6

The restaurant is on the _____. It's _____ the bank and the
                               7   8

movie theater.

B **Real-life math** Look at the map. Complete the sentences.

How far is it?

1. It's ____107____ miles from San Diego to Los Angeles.

2. It's _____ miles from Los Angeles to San Jose.

3. It's _____ miles from San Jose to San Francisco.

4. It's _____ miles from San Diego to San Francisco.

A **Read the questions. Circle *yes* or *no*.**

1. Do you have an emergency exit map for your home?　　yes　　no
2. Are you prepared for a fire or an accident?　　yes　　no

B **Read the poster.**

Emergency

Fire

Is there a fire?

1. Call 911.

2. Give your address, name, and phone number.

3. Give the location of the fire.

4. Exit the building.

🚪**EXIT**

Help

Accident

Is there an accident?

1. Call 911.

2. Give your address, name, and phone number.

3. Give the location of the accident.

4. Wait for help.

C **Look at the poster in B. Circle *a* or *b*.**

1. There's a fire. _____ 911.
   a. Give
   (b.) Call

2. Give your address, name, and _____.
   a. phone number
   b. age

3. _____ the building.
   a. Exit
   b. Cali

4. There's an accident. Call _____.
   a. help
   b. 911

5. Give the _____ of the accident.
   a. time
   b. location

6. Wait for _____.
   a. help
   b. 911

A Complete the sentences. Use the words in the box.

| There | ~~many~~ | between | across | clinic | station |
| office | school | fire | bus | bank | |

Across

2. How ____many____ restaurants are there?

4. There's a _____ stop on the right.

7. _____ are three cars on the road.

8. The _____ station is on the left.

10. Take the car to the gas _____.

11. He's sick. He's at the _____.

Down

1. The pharmacy is _____ the restaurant and the parking lot.

3. The pharmacy is _____ from the park.

5. We are studying at _____.

6. Is there a post _____ here?

9. I'm taking the check to the _____.

B Write the words in the crossword puzzle.

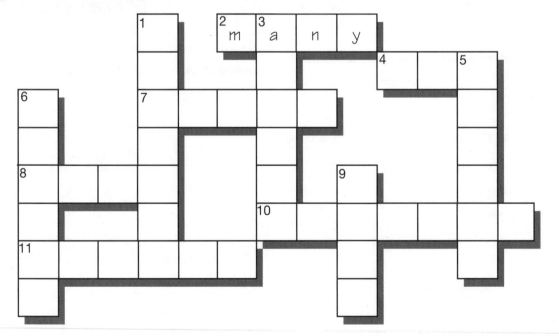

UNIT 6

Daily Routines

Vocabulary

A Look at the pictures. Read the activities. Check (✓) the activities you do at home. Mark (X) activities you do at work or at school. Some activities may have both a ✓ and an X.

At home

At school

do homework _____	get up _____	go to bed ___✓___	do housework _____
have lunch _____	study ✓+ X	make dinner _____	ride the bus _____
drink coffee _____	work _____	take a shower _____	come home _____

B Choose 4 activities you do at home. Complete the sentences about the activities. Give the times.

I eat lunch at 12:30 p.m.

1. I _____ at _____ .

2. I _____ at _____ .

3. I _____ at _____ .

4. I _____ at _____ .

C Choose 3 activities you do at work or school. Complete the sentences about the activities. Give the times.

I study math at 9 a.m.

1. I _____ at _____ .

2. I _____ at _____ .

3. I _____ at _____ .

A Read the work schedule.

Hotel Royale	
Daily Work Schedule: Oscar LaPlante	
2nd Shift: 4:00 p.m. to 12:00 a.m. Work days: Thursday to Sunday	
Time	**Job**
4:00 p.m. to 6:00 p.m.	vacuum the rugs
6:00 p.m. to 8:00 p.m.	mop the floors
8:00 p.m. to 8:30 p.m.	eat dinner
8:30 p.m. to 12:00 a.m.	wash the tables/ help the manager

B Look at the work schedule in A. Complete the sentences.

1. My name is Oscar LaPlante. I work at the _____ Hotel Royale _____.

2. I work four days a week, from Thursday to _____.

3. I work from _____ to midnight.

4. I _____ from 4:00 to 6:00.

5. From 6:00 to 8:00, I _____.

6. I _____ at 8:00 with my friend Alfredo.

7. At 8:30, I _____ and help _____.

8. I go home at _____. My family is sleeping!

C Check (✓) the things you do at work or at home. Then choose 3 activities. Write sentences. Write the day and time.

At work or at home?					
	Work	**Home**		**Work**	**Home**
wash windows		(✓)	mop the floor		
vacuum rugs			answer the phone		
use a copy machine			have lunch		

I wash windows on Saturday at noon.

1. _____

2. _____

3. _____

A Look at the pictures. Read the days. Complete the sentences.

Linda

Pat

Maria and Lisa

Saturday and Sunday   Tuesday and Thursday   Monday and Tuesday

1. On Saturday and Sunday, Linda _____visits_____ a friend.

2. On Monday and Tuesday, Maria _____ TV.

3. Lisa _____ on Monday and Tuesday.

4. Pat _____ the kids to the park on Tuesday and Thursday.

5. He _____ with the kids in the park.

6. Linda _____ in the park on Saturday and Sunday.

B Read Linda's paragraph.

    I live in San Jose. I work on the weekends. I ride the bus to work in the morning. Some days, I visit a friend after work. Her name is Judy. We listen to music and talk for hours. We exercise in the park.

C Look at the paragraph in B. Answer the information questions. Use complete sentences and the simple present.

1. Where does Linda live?

   Linda lives in San Jose.

2. When does she work?

   _____

3. When does she ride the bus?

   _____

4. When does she visit Judy?

   _____

D Complete the questions about Jon and Monica. Use *do* or *does*. Then answer the questions.

8 a.m. to 4 p.m.

8 a.m. to 4 p.m.

4 p.m. to 6 p.m.

6 p.m. to 7 p.m.

8 p.m. to 10 p.m.

8 p.m. to 2 a.m.

1. When ____does____ Jon work? _He works from 8 a.m. to 4 p.m._____

2. When _____ Monica do housework? _____

3. When _____ they exercise? _____

4. When _____ they eat dinner? _____

5. When _____ Jon do housework? _____

6. When _____ Monica work? _____

E 🚀 Grammar Boost   Complete the questions. Use *do*, *does*, *is*, or *are*. Then match the questions with the answers.

_c_ 1. _Does_____ Jim have a brother?   a. No, I'm not.

____ 2. _____ you eat lunch at 12:00?   b. No, he isn't.

____ 3. _____ you at home?   c. Yes, he does.

____ 4. _____ he at work right now?   d. No, they don't.

____ 5. _____ they in this class?   e. Yes, I do.

____ 6. _____ they arrive on time?   f. No, they aren't.

A Match the pictures with the sentences.

 a
 b
 c
 d

__d__ 1. Put the paper in the printer.

____ 2. Push this button.

____ 3. Fill the stapler.

____ 4. Turn on the computer.

B Complete the conversation. Use the words in the box.

problem	the paper here	help me	my job	~~Excuse me~~	fill the

A: _Excuse me_____, Ms. Jones. Can you _____?
　　　　　　1　　　　　　　　　　　　　　　　　　　　　2

B: Yes? What is it?

A: How do I _____ copy machine?
　　　　　　　　　　3

B: Let me see. Put _____.
　　　　　　　　　　　　　4

A: Oh. Thank you.

B: No _____. That's _____.
　　　　　5　　　　　　　　　　　　　　　　　　6

C Add -s or -es. Rewrite the verbs.

1. wash　　→　_washes_____

2. play　　→　_____

3. fix　　　→　_____

4. watch　→　_____

5. work　　→　_____

6. exercise →　_____

A **Read the article.**

Family Time

Is the family important? Is there time for family?

Look at the number of hours in a day. Do parents have time to spend with their children? Many parents work for about ten hours each day. They do housework and sleep for about ten hours. There are four hours left for the children.

The children have homework. They like computers, television, and video games. There are only about two hours left for the family.

Is the family important? Yes, it is! Is there time for the family? That is the question!

B **Look at the article in A. Circle *a* or *b*.**

1. Who works?
   a. children
   b. parents *(circled)*

2. How many hours do people work each day?
   a. 4
   b. 10

3. What do children have at night?
   a. homework
   b. housework

4. How many hours are left for families?
   a. 2
   b. 10

5. This article says ____.
   a. families aren't important
   b. families need more time

C **Answer the questions. Use your own information. Use complete sentences.**

How many hours do you work? I work 7 hours every day.

1. How many hours do you work?

   _____

2. How many hours do you sleep at night?

   _____

3. How many hours do you spend with your family?

   _____

A Unscramble the words. Complete the sentences.

1. At work, I ___answer___ the phone. (sranwe)

2. We _____ home from work at 5:30 p.m. (meco)

3. They _____ the windows in the morning. (ashw)

4. What time do you _____ up? (egt)

5. I _____ coffee in the morning. (knird)

6. We _____ at school. (dsuty)

7. At work, they _____ the manager. (phel)

8. At 7:00 p.m., I _____ dinner. (aekm)

B Write the words from A in the puzzle.

8:00 AM
9:30 AM   1.   _a_ _n_ |_s_| _w_ _e_ _r_
6:00 PM   2. |__| __ __ __
7:30 PM   3. __ __ __ |__|
6:00 AM
8:30 AM   4.   __ |__| __
5:00 PM   5. |__| __ __ __ __
1:30 PM   6.   __ __ |__| __ __
7:00 AM
8:30 AM   7.   __ __ |__| __
4:00 PM   8. __ __ __ |__|
5:30 PM

C Look at the letters in the boxes in B. What's the secret word?

$\underset{1}{\underline{s}}$ $\underset{2}{\underline{}}$ $\underset{3}{\underline{}}$ $\underset{4}{\underline{}}$ $\underset{5}{\underline{}}$ $\underset{6}{\underline{}}$ $\underset{7}{\underline{}}$ $\underset{8}{\underline{}}$

Shop and Spend

A Match the amounts of money with the pictures.

①   ②   ③    ④

⑤   ⑥   ⑦   ⑧

| ____ 25¢ | ____ $5.00 | ____ $1.00 | ____ 75¢ |
| ____ 1¢ | _1_ 5¢ | ____ 10¢ | ____ 50¢ |

B Look at the pictures. Answer the questions. Use complete sentences.

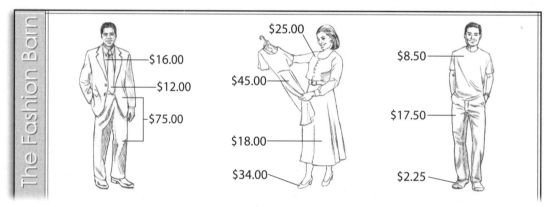

The Fashion Barn

- Suit: $16.00, $12.00, $75.00
- Dress: $25.00, $45.00, $18.00, $34.00
- T-shirt: $8.50, $17.50, $2.25

1. How much is the T-shirt?

   It's $8.50.

2. How much is the tie?

   _____

3. How much are the woman's shoes?

   _____

4. How much is the suit?

   _____

5. How much is the dress?

   _____

6. How much are the socks?

   _____

7. How much are the pants?

   _____

8. How much is the blouse?

   _____

A **Read the ads.**

A

Spring Dresses
are Here!
❀ ❀ ❀ ❀

*For those special
occasions...*

We accept credit cards and checks.

B

**Back to School
SALE**

*Our prices are
very good!*

Cash only!

B **Look at the ads in A. Where is each customer? Write *A* or *B*.**

_B_ 1. "The prices are good!"

____ 2. "This dress is too expensive!"

____ 3. "I'm using my credit card today."

____ 4. "I'm writing a check."

____ 5. "This is perfect, and it's on sale!"

____ 6. "Oh, dear! I don't have any cash with me."

C **Look at Saera's chart. Answer the questions. Use complete sentences.**

What Does Saera Wear?

At home	At work	On special occasions
jeans	uniform	blouse
sweater	hat	skirt

1. What does Saera wear at home? _She wears jeans and a sweater._

2. What does she wear at work? _____

3. What does she wear on special occasions? _____

A **Match the questions with the answers.**

_c_ 1. Do you want a new car?   a. No, she doesn't.

____ 2. Do we need a new car?   b. Yes, they do.

____ 3. Does Philippe have a jacket?   c. Yes, I do.

____ 4. Does Sharon need some paper?   d. Yes, you do.

____ 5. Do Mark and Adam have books?   e. Yes, he does.

____ 6. Do I need a sweater today?   f. No, we don't.

B **Complete the questions. Use *do* or *does*. Then answer the questions.**

1. **A:** _Does_____ Sharon like to shop?

   B: Yes, _____ _she does_____.

2. **A:** _____ Sharon want to buy the skirt?

   B: No, _____.

3. **A:** _____ Roberto have a credit card?

   B: No, _____.

4. **A:** _____ Roberto need a jacket?

   B: Yes, _____.

5. **A:** _____ the salespeople help the customers?

   B: Yes, _____.

6. **A:** _____ you like to shop?

   B: Yes, _____.

C Look at the pictures. Complete the sentences. Use *need, want,* or *have*.

1. Hetal and his wife ___have___ a small apartment.

2. They _____ to buy a new house.

3. They _____ a lot of money for the house.

4. Nancy _____ a bicycle.

5. She _____ a new car.

6. Nancy _____ $20,000 for the car.

D Write simple present *Yes/No* questions. Use the words in parentheses.

1. **A:** _Do the children need new jackets?_ (the children / need / new jackets)

   B: No, they need new shoes.

2. **A:** _____ (John / want / a new house)

   B: No, he has a nice apartment.

3. **A:** _____ (Sara / want / the blue blouse)

   B: No, she wants the red blouse.

4. **A:** _____ (you / want / the green sweater)

   B: No, I don't like it.

E 🚀 Grammar Boost Complete the questions and answers. Use *do, does, have,* or *has*.

1. **A:** _Does_ Ana have some cash?

   B: No, but she ___has___ a check.

2. **A:** _____ Sara and Philippe have a check?

   B: No, but they _____ a credit card.

3. **A:** _____ your friends have a new house?

   B: No, but they _____ a new car.

4. **A:** _____ your neighbor have a new car?

   B: No, he doesn't _____ a new car.

A **Complete the conversation. Use the words in the box.**

Here's	take it	~~Excuse~~	How much	What size	on sale

A: Excuse _____ me. _____ is this shirt?
              1   2

B: It's _____ for $14.95. _____ do you need?
              3   4

A: I need a small.

B: _____ a small in blue.
              5

A: Okay. I'll _____.
              6

B **Look at the order form. Answer the questions. Use complete sentences.**

Item	Item Number	Size	Color	Price	Number	Total
sweater	210543	M	White	16.95	2	$33.90
gloves	712288	M	Green	12.95	1	$12.95
jacket	342995	L	Blue	24.95	1	$24.95

1. What color are the sweaters? _They're white._

2. How much is one sweater? _____

3. How many sweaters does the customer want? _____

4. How much are the gloves? _____

5. What size is the jacket? _____

C **Real-life math** **Look at the receipts. How much is the change? Write the amounts.**

Save More! THANK YOU <<<>>>		*Save More!* THANK YOU <<<>>>		*Save More!* THANK YOU <<<>>>	
Store#:006	Register #:03	Store#:006	Register #:03	Store#:006	Register #:01
Pants	$20.95	Pants	$15.95	Pants	$23.95
Tax	$ 1.68	Tax	$ 1.28	Tax	$ 1.92
Total	$22.63	Total	$17.23	Total	$25.87
Cash	$30.00	Cash	$20.00	Cash	$40.00
Change	$7.37	Change	$_____	Change	$_____
>>><<<		>>><<<		>>><<<	

A Read the brochure.

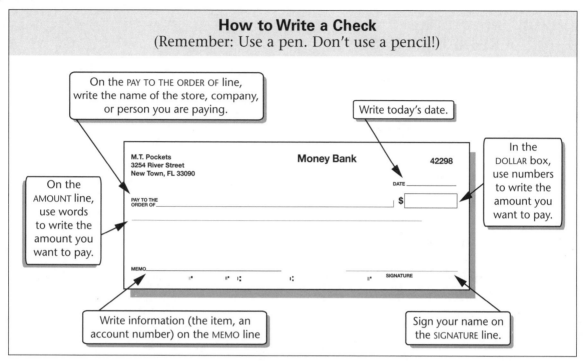

How to Write a Check
(Remember: Use a pen. Don't use a pencil!)

On the PAY TO THE ORDER OF line, write the name of the store, company, or person you are paying.

Write today's date.

On the AMOUNT line, use words to write the amount you want to pay.

In the DOLLAR box, use numbers to write the amount you want to pay.

M.T. Pockets
3254 River Street
New Town, FL 33090

Money Bank

42298

DATE _____

PAY TO THE
ORDER OF _____

$ _____

MEMO _____

SIGNATURE _____

Write information (the item, an account number) on the MEMO line

Sign your name on the SIGNATURE line.

B Look at the brochure in A. Circle the correct words.

1. Use a (pencil / (pen)) to write a check.

2. Write the store or company on the (PAY TO THE ORDER OF / SIGNATURE) line.

3. Use (words / numbers) to write the amount in the DOLLAR box.

4. Sign your name on the (AMOUNT / SIGNATURE) line.

C You are at Super Store. You are buying a radio. It costs $32.45. Complete the check.

M.T. Pockets
3254 River Street
New Town, FL 33090

Money Bank

42298

DATE _____

PAY TO THE
ORDER OF _____

$ _____

MEMO _____

SIGNATURE _____

A Circle the letter of the correct answer.

A SECRET MESSAGE

1. How much is the blouse?
   I. $15   **B.** Small

2. What color do you want?
   A. Yes, I do.   **T.** Blue

3. Does Tomas need a jacket?
   R. Yes, they do.   **S.** No, he doesn't.

4. What size do you need?
   O. Medium   **P.** It's perfect.

5. Are there any shoes on sale?
   N. Yes, there are.   **O.** Yes, there is.

6. What do you wear at home?
   U. Yes, I do.   **S.** Jeans and a T-shirt

7. Is there an ATM in the store?
   A. Yes, there is.   **B.** No, it isn't.

8. Do Mike and Sara have a new car?
   K. Yes, he does.   **L.** No, they don't.

9. How much are the socks?
   I. It's $4.   **E.** They're $3.50.

B Write the letters from the answers in A. Read the message.

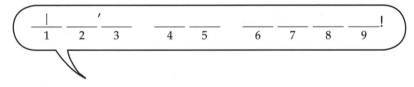

I __ __' __ __ __ __ __ __ __ __ __!
1   2   3   4   5   6   7   8   9

UNIT 8

Eating Well

LESSON 1   Vocabulary

A   **Complete the sentences. Use the words in the box.**

~~cart~~   basket   checker   bagger   aisle

1. Joe is buying a lot of food. He's using a _____cart_____.

2. Rita is only buying two or three things. She has a small _____.

3. The _____ is putting the potatoes into a bag.

4. The bread is in _____ 1, next to the cookies.

5. The _____ is working at the cash register.

B   **Match the words with the pictures.**

①   ②   ③

④   ⑤   ⑥

⑦   ⑧   ⑨

___ bananas   ___ milk   ___ potatoes   ___ apples   ___ lettuce

___ tomatoes   ___ eggs   _1_ grapes   ___ onions

C   **Circle *a* or *b*.**

1. A ____ works in a supermarket.
   a.) bagger   b. customer

2. People use ____ in the store.
   a. baskets   b. cars

3. Onions and ____ are vegetables.
   a. bread   b. lettuce

4. Grapes and bananas are ____.
   a. vegetables   b. fruit

LESSON 2 Life stories

A Complete the sentences. Use the words in the box.

a customer	~~a cashier~~	good prices
a shopping list	once a week	is buying

1. My name is Sasha. I work here at Save More Supermarket.
   I'm _____ a cashier _____.

2. Here comes Mr. Singh. He's _____ here.

3. He brings _____ with him every time he shops.

4. Today he _____ fruit, vegetables, and fish.

5. Mr. Singh buys fish _____. We have fresh fish every Thursday.

6. Mr. Singh is a good shopper. He always looks for _____.

B Look at the pictures. Write the shopping list for each person. Use the words in the box.

bananas	bread	potatoes	chicken	cookies	fish
eggs	~~lettuce~~	milk	ice cream	soup	grapes

lettuce

A Read the calendar.

October 2006

Sunday	Monday	Tuesday	Wednesday	Thursday	Friday	Saturday
1 exercise, study	**2** work, exercise	**3** work, exercise, visit Louis	**4** work, exercise, cook dinner	**5** shopping, exercise, cook dinner	**6** visit parents, exercise	**7** clean apt., shopping, exercise
8	**9**	**10**	**11**	**12**	**13**	**14**

B Look at the calendar in A. Complete the sentences. Use the words in the box.

~~three times~~   twice a week   never   every day

1. Helen works _____three times_____ a week.

2. She exercises _____.

3. Helen goes shopping _____.

4. Helen _____ eats out on Wednesdays.

C Unscramble the sentences.

1. dinner / cook / We / at / always / home
   We always cook dinner at home.

2. ice cream / eat / I / never
   _____

3. Paula / a / once / pizza / eats / week
   _____

4. month / friends / times / They / a / have/ with / dinner / four
   _____

D Complete the sentences. Use your own information.

I cook dinner six times a week.

1. I cook dinner _____.

2. I order pizza _____.

3. I eat dinner with friends _____.

E Look at the chart. Read the questions. Check (✔) the correct answers. Use your own information.

How Often Do You Do These Things?

	every day	once a week	once a month	once or twice a year	never
1. How often do you go shopping?					
2. How often do you eat fish?					
3. How often do you eat lunch with your family?					
4. How often do you go to a restaurant for breakfast?					

F Look at the chart in E. Write sentences.

I go shopping once a week.

1. _____

2. _____

3. _____

4. _____

G **Grammar Boost**   Read the Grammar note. Then write sentences with *always, often, sometimes,* or *never*. Use your own information.

Grammar note

always	often	sometimes	never
100%	70%	30%	0%

I often study English in the evening.

1. study English / the evening

   _____

2. ride / the bus

   _____

3. get up / 7 a.m.

   _____

4. go to bed / 8 p.m.

   _____

A Complete the conversation. Use the words in the box.

~~ready to order~~	I'd like	that's one	anything to drink
I do	coffee too	right	please

Server: Are you _____ready to order_____?
                            1

Beena: Yes, we are. _____ a
                              2

chicken sandwich, _____.
                                3

Server: Do you want _____?
                              4

Beena: Yes, _____. I'd like some
                        5

coffee.

Server: And you?

Carl: Some vegetable soup and a salad. No onions in the salad, please.

Server: Anything to drink?

Carl: I'd like _____, please.
                        6

Server: Okay, _____ chicken sandwich, vegetable soup
                        7

and a salad with no onions, and two cups of coffee.

Beena: That's _____.
                        8

B Look at the conversation in A. Write Carl and Beena's order. Use the prices on the menu. How much is their lunch? Write the total.

Home Cooking Coffee Shop
ORDER

Quantity	Item	Price
1	chicken sandwich	$6.95
	Total:	
	Thank You!	

Home Cooking Coffee Shop
— MENU —

Sandwiches—$6.95
*Cheese and Tomato
Chicken or Beef*

Soup—$3.95
*Chicken and Rice
Vegetable*

Salad—$4.95

Coffee or Tea—$1.50

A Read the article.

Is Pizza Healthy?

Many people say, "Pizza is not a healthy food." Other people say, "Pizza is good for you." Think about it. Pizza can be good for you.

- Order pizza with vegetables on it.
  You can order pizza with tomatoes, peppers, onions, and mushrooms.

- Don't order pizza with pepperoni. Order pizza with chicken. Pepperoni has a lot salt, but chicken doesn't. A lot of salt is unhealthy.

- Some places have pizza with pineapple on it. Pineapple is a fruit. Order pineapple pizza to be healthy.

So you see, pizza can be a healthy food!

Pineapples

B Look at the article in A. Circle *a* or *b*.

1. Pizza with vegetables on it is _____.
   a. healthy
   b. unhealthy

2. Sue wants pizza with vegetables.
   She can order _____.
   a. pizza with peppers and mushrooms
   b. pizza with chicken and pineapple

3. Paul wants pizza with only a
   little salt. He can order _____.
   a. pizza with pepperoni
   b. pizza with chicken

4. Pineapple pizza is _____.
   a. healthy
   b. unhealthy

5. Pizza is _____ healthy.
   a. always
   b. sometimes

Find the Differences

Look at the pictures. Alicia and Frank do different things for lunch on Thursdays and Fridays. Find the differences. Complete the sentences.

1. On Thursdays, Alicia and Frank eat lunch at ___12 p.m.___

   On Fridays, they eat lunch at ___1 p.m.___

2. On Thursdays, Alicia drinks _____.

   On Fridays, she drinks _____.

3. On Thursdays, Frank eats _____.

   On Fridays, he eats _____ and a _____.

4. On Thursdays, Alicia eats _____, french fries, and a _____.

   On Fridays, she eats _____ and a _____.

5. On Thursdays, Frank drinks a _____ soda.

   On Fridays, he drinks a _____ soda.

Your Health

A Look at the picture. Match the words with the picture. Use the words in the box.

| ~~mouth~~ | leg | head | arm | neck | nose | foot | hand | chest |

1. ___mouth___   4. _____   7. _____

2. _____   5. _____   8. _____

3. _____   6. _____   9. _____

B Look at the picture in A. Complete the sentences. Use the words in the box.

| doctor | fever | receptionist | earache | ~~patient~~ | nurse |

1. What's the matter with the _____patient_____?

2. He has an _____.

3. He has a _____, too.

4. The _____ is looking at his ear.

5. The _____ is answering the telephone.

6. The _____ is helping the doctor.

A **Complete the story. Use the words in the box.**

examines her	drinks some	to the doctor	her temperature	a prescription
~~sick~~	sore throat	goes home	the medicine	

Kim is _____sick_____ today. She has a fever and a
              1
_____. She goes _____. The
         2   3
doctor _____ and takes _____.
                      4   5
The doctor writes _____. Kim
                                    6
_____. At home, she takes _____
                7   8
and _____ hot tea.
              9

B **How do you get better? Check (✓) the things you do. Then write sentences.**

What do you do for a...	rest	drink fluids	take medicine	exercise
1. cold?	✓	✓		
2. backache?				
3. headache?				
4. stomachache?				
5. earache?				
6. fever?				

For a cold, I rest and drink fluids.

1. _____

2. _____

3. _____

4. _____

5. _____

6. _____

A **Complete the sentences. Use *has* or *have*.**

1. I _____have_____ a headache.

2. Kim _____ a sore throat.

3. We _____ to exercise every day.

4. The doctor and nurse _____ a lot of work today.

5. You _____ to quit smoking.

6. He _____ to stay home and rest.

B **Complete the sentences. Use *have/has* or *have to/has to*.**

1. I _____have_____ a headache. I ___have to___ rest.

2. Lily _____ go to the dentist. She _____ a toothache.

3. Paul _____ a broken leg. He _____ stay home.

4. They _____ drink fluids and rest. They _____ colds.

5. You _____ a fever. You _____ go to the doctor.

C **Unscramble the questions. Then complete the answers. Use *have/has* or *have to/has to*.**

1. you / have / study / to / do / Why

   A: _Why do you have to study?_____

   B: I _____have_____ a test tomorrow.

2. does / take / Why / he / have / to / medicine

   A: _____

   B: He _____ a cold.

3. they / store / Why / do / to / go / to / have / the

   A: _____

   B: They _____ buy some food.

4. every / day / Why / she / does / have / to / run

   A: _____

   B: She _____ exercise.

5. do / Why / leave / have / you / early / to

   A: _____

   B: I _____ pick up my son.

D Complete the questions.

1. **A:** Where _does John have to go?_ _____
   B: John has to go to the pharmacy.

2. **A:** What _____
   B: He has to buy some medicine.

3. **A:** Where _____
   B: They have to go to school tomorrow.

4. **A:** When _____
   B: You have to go to bed at 11 p.m.

5. **A:** How often _____
   B: She has to take the pills twice a day.

E 🚀 Grammar Boost   Look at the chart. Then rewrite the sentences. Change *have/has* to *have got/has got*.

> ### *Have got* and *have got to*
>
> In conversation people often use *have got* or *has got* instead of *have* or *has*. The meaning is the same.
>
> | | |
> |---|---|
> | I **have got** a cold. = I **have** a cold. | I **have got** to work. = I **have to** work. |
> | Pam **has got** a test. = Pam **has** a test. | She **has got** to study. = She **has to** study. |

1. We have some good friends.

   We have got some good friends. _____

2. You have a nice family.

   _____

3. The teacher has to leave early tonight.

   _____

4. They have to work this weekend.

   _____

5. I have to stay home. I have a fever.

   _____

6. You have to exercise more.

   _____

A Read the appointment card. Answer the questions.

1. Who has an appointment?

   Rick DeSoto.

2. What day is the appointment?

   _____

3. What time is the appointment?

   _____

4. What's the date of the appointment?

   _____

Dentist Appointment

Patient: ___Rick DeSoto_____

Has an appointment on: _Monday, May 23_

At: _11:00_____ (a.m.) p.m.

With: _____Dr. Silver_____

Please call (978) 555-3730
to cancel your appointment

B Complete the conversation. Use the words in the box.

it is	9 a.m.	Tuesday, October 5th
~~see the dentist~~	that okay	has an opening

A: Can I help you?

B: My name is Karen Hill. I have to _____see the dentist_____ in six months.
                                              1

A: Let's see. Dr. Durgin _____ on October 5th at 9 a.m.
                                  2

   Is _____?
          3

B: Yes, _____. Thanks.
               4

A: Okay. See you on _____ at _____.
                            5   6

C Look at the conversation in B. Complete the appointment card.

Dentist Appointment

Patient: _____

Has an appointment on: _____

At: _____ a.m. p.m.

With: _____

Please call (978) 555-3730 to cancel your appointment

A Read the article.

Health Note of the Day

Chicken Soup:
It's Good Medicine!

← Steam

My grandmother says chicken soup is good for people with colds. Now doctors are finding that chicken soup is good medicine. The hot steam helps you. There are onions, carrots, and other vegetables in chicken soup that help you. Bananas, oranges, and tea are good for colds, too.

Do you have a cold? Listen to your grandmother! Have some chicken soup.

B Look at the article in A. Mark the sentences T (true) or F (false).

__T__ 1. The writer's grandmother says chicken soup is good for colds.

_____ 2. Now doctors think that chicken soup is bad for colds.

_____ 3. The steam of the soup can help.

_____ 4. The fruit in chicken soup helps you.

_____ 5. You have a cold. You should call your grandmother.

C Read the medicine label. Answer the questions.

1. How many pills does she take every day?

   _two_____

2. How often does she take this medicine?

   _____

3. Should she take this medicine with food?

   _____

4. How many refills are there?

   _____

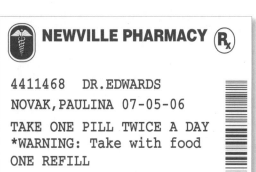

NEWVILLE PHARMACY ℞

4411468   DR.EDWARDS
NOVAK,PAULINA 07-05-06

TAKE ONE PILL TWICE A DAY
*WARNING: Take with food
ONE REFILL

A Go around the spiral. Find 8 things a doctor says. Write them on the lines below. Use complete sentences.

1. _Go home and drink juice._
2. _____
3. _____
4. _____
5. _____
6. _____
7. _____
8. _____

B Create your own "sentence spiral." Bring it to class. Then ask your classmates to find the sentences.

LESSON 1   Vocabulary

A   **Who says these things? Write the jobs. Use the words in the box.**

childcare worker   ~~server~~   janitor   plumber   delivery person   cook

1. I serve food in a restaurant.   server

2. I clean the floors and fix things.   _____

3. I take care of children.   _____

4. I make food in a restaurant.   _____

5. I deliver packages.   _____

6. I fix sinks.   _____

B   **What do they do? Where do they work? Complete the sentences with the job and the place.**

1. Yolanda's a _____gardener_____.

    She works in a _____.

2. Mark's a _____.

    He works in a _____.

A **Read the help-wanted ads. Answer the questions.**

1. What's the job in ad A?

   server

2. Is this job full-time or part-time?

   _____

3. Is the job in the mornings or in the evenings?

   _____

4. What's the job in ad B?

   _____

5. Where is the job?

   _____

6. Is this a full-time or part-time job?

   _____

A

┌─── **Help Wanted** ───┐

Lisa's Restaurant is looking for servers.
Evenings, PT (18 hours a week).
Call Fred: 555-1302

B

┌─── **Help Wanted** ───┐

Childcare Worker at Children's Castle
FT (40 hours a week). Call Danielle for
an application: 555-2212

B **Read the story. Complete the sentences. Use the words in the box.**

| as a bus driver | in person | Internet | interview for the job |
| full-time | ~~job~~ | help-wanted ads | completes a form |

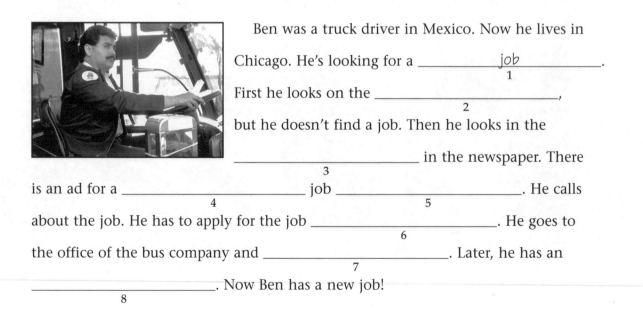

Ben was a truck driver in Mexico. Now he lives in

Chicago. He's looking for a _____job_____.
                                      1

First he looks on the _____,
                                 2

but he doesn't find a job. Then he looks in the

_____ in the newspaper. There
              3

is an ad for a _____ job _____. He calls
                        4   5

about the job. He has to apply for the job _____. He goes to
                                                          6

the office of the bus company and _____. Later, he has an
                                                   7

_____. Now Ben has a new job!
              8

A Look at the timeline. Complete the sentences. Use *was* or *were*.
(not) = make sentence negative.

1985	1999	2001	2005
POLAND		**NEW JERSEY**	

Stan- *student* Stan- *cook* Stan- *cook*
Marie- *student* Marie- *nurse* Marie- *homemaker*

In 1985, Stan and I ___were___ in Poland.
1
Stan _____ a student for 14 years. I
2
_____ also a student. From 1999 to 2001, we _____
3   4
(not) students. I _____ a nurse, and Stan _____ a
5   6
cook. In 2002, we _____ (not) in Poland. We _____
7   8
in New Jersey.

B Look at the timeline in A. Complete the questions. Use *was* or *were*.
Write short answers.

1. A: _Was_ Stan a student in 2003?
   B: _No, he wasn't._

2. A: _____ Stan and Maria in Poland in 2000?
   B: _____

3. A: _____ they in school from 1999 to 2005?
   B: _____

4. A: _____ Maria a nurse from 2001 to 2005?
   B: _____

5. A: In 1990, _____ Stan a cook?
   B: _____

6. A: _____ they in New Jersey in 2004?
   B: _____

C **Write sentences. Use the simple past with *be*.**

1. Min and Hung-ju / students / in Korea

   <u>Min and Hung-ju were students in Korea.</u>

2. They / students / from 1995 to 2001

   _____

3. Min / a nurse / from 2001 to 2003

   _____

4. Hung-ju / not / a teacher / in Korea

   _____

5. Min and Hung-ju / in San Francisco / last year

   _____

6. Min / not / in Korea / last year

   _____

D 🚀 **Grammar Boost**   **Read about Ana. Then complete the questions and short answers. Use *is*, *was*, or *does*. Use complete sentences.**

> Ana was a student in El Salvador for 14 years, from 1985 to 1999. After that, she was a teacher for four years in the capital city, San Salvador. She was there from 2000 to 2004. Then she was in Florida for one year. Now, she's in Arlington, Virginia. She has a job. She's a childcare worker.

1. **A:** <u>Was</u>_____ Ana a student in El Salvador?

   B: <u>Yes, she was.</u>_____

2. **A:** _____ she a teacher in San Salvador for four years?

   B: _____

3. **A:** _____ she in Florida for two years?

   B: _____

4. **A:** _____ she in Florida now?

   B: _____

5. **A:** _____ she have a job now?

   B: _____

A Complete the conversation. Use the words in the box.

You're hired	can use	I do	an office manager
I can	work experience	~~Tell me~~	weekends

A: <u>Tell me</u> about yourself, Ms. Singh.
           1

B: I'm from India. I lived there for 25 years.

A: Do you have any _____?
                            2

B: Yes, _____. I was _____ from 1999
              3   4

   to 2005 in India. In 2006, I was an office worker in Charleston.

   I _____ a computer and photocopier. I like to work with people.
              5

A: Can you work _____?
                    6

B: Yes, _____.
           7

A: That's great. _____.
              8

B Look at the conversation in A. Complete the application form.

JOB APPLICATION

Position: <u>Office Manager</u> **Applicant Name:** <u>Anita Singh</u>

Experience:

Job Title	Number of Years	Location
_____	_____	<u>India</u>
_____	_____	<u>Charleston</u>

Skills: Please check (✓) the skills you have

_____ use a computer	_____ drive	_____ fix office machines
_____ make copies	_____ answer phones	_____ other

A Read the article and the timecard.

On the Job and On time

Good employees come to work on time every day. They don't leave early. This is very important at the Top Star Hotel. The Top Star employees use a time clock and timecards. They have to use the time clock twice a day. This means they put their cards into the time clock when they come to work and when they leave. At the end of each week, the employees give their cards to the boss. The boss knows how many hours they work each week. This is an example of a timecard from the Top Star Hotel.

Top Star Hotel

EMPLOYEE TIMECARD

Name: Lucy Harvie   Employee No.: 0923

Week of: June 2   to June 8

Date	In/Out	Time
06-03	Time in:	03:00 p.m.
06-03	Time out:	10:00 p.m.
06-05	Time in:	03:00 p.m.
06-05	Time out:	10:00 p.m.
06-08	Time in:	02:30 p.m.
06-08	Time out:	10:30 p.m.
	Total Hours:	22
	Rate:	$12.50

B Look at the article in A. Mark the sentences T (true) or F (false).

__T__ 1. Good employees are on time for work every day.

_____ 2. Good employees often leave early.

_____ 3. The Top Star Hotel employees use a time clock.

_____ 4. At the end of each week, employees take their timecards home.

_____ 5. Lucy Harvie often gets to work at 3:00 p.m.

_____ 6. On June 5, Lucy was at work at 9:00 p.m.

_____ 7. From June 3 to June 8, Lucy was at work for 22 hours.

_____ 8. On June 8, Lucy was not at work at 1:00 p.m.

A **Unscramble the words.**

Jobs and Work Places

1. c h a m e i c n   <u>mechanic</u>
2. e r g a g a   _____
3. r e v e r s   _____
4. t e s t a r n u a r   _____
5. d e n s r a g   _____
6. d a r n e r e g   _____
7. c o o l s h   _____
8. r a t i j o n   _____

B **Complete the chart. Use the words in the box.**

janitor	office	kitchen	manager	gardener	garage
garden	restaurant	school	cook	server	~~mechanic~~

Jobs	Workplaces	Skills
mechanic		fixes cars
		cleans buildings
		plants flowers
		serves food
		cooks food
		manages a business

C **Write sentences. Use the information in the chart.**

1. <u>A mechanic works in a garage and fixes cars.</u>
2. _____
3. _____
4. _____
5. _____
6. _____

Safety First

LESSON 1 Vocabulary

A Look at the pictures. Write the words. Use the words in the box.

| stop   road work   school crossing   ~~no parking~~   no left turn   speed limit |

1. _no parking_   3. _____   5. _____

2. _____   4. _____   6. _____

B Cross out (X) the item that does NOT belong in each group.

1. safety boots   hard hat   fire extinguisher   ~~wet floor~~

2. careless   safety glasses unsafe   dangerous

3. white   orange   safe   black

4. safety boots   factory worker safety gloves   hard hat

C Complete the sentences. Use the words in the box.

| dangerous   careless   emergency exit   ~~careful~~ |

1. Matt is _____careful_____. He wears a hard hat.

2. Savan doesn't wear a hard hat. She is _____.

3. That building is not safe. It's _____!

4. We have to leave the building. Where's the _____?

A Look at the picture. Check (✓) the rules people are following. Mark (X) the rules people are not following.

_____ 1. Be careful with chemicals.

_____ 2. Wear safety boots.

_____ 3. Don't walk on a wet floor.

_____ 4. Wear a hard hat.

_____ 5. Wear safety glasses.

_____ 6. Wear safety gloves.

B Complete the sentences. Use the words in the box.

slow down   going fast   ~~always wears~~   check the speed   careful

Nate is going to work. He ___*always wears*___ his seatbelt in the car.
                                                    1
Today, he is late for work, and he is _____. He sees the
                                                    2
sign for the school, but he doesn't _____. Nate doesn't
                                                    3
_____ limit. He also doesn't see the police officer. The police
           4
officer stops Nate. Now he is _____ near a school.
                                                    5

C 🖩 **Real-life math** Answer the questions.

In a small factory, there are 100 workers. Fifteen of the 100 workers don't wear safety boots. They often have accidents on the wet floors.

1. What percent of the workers don't wear safety boots? _15_%

2. What percent of the workers wear safety boots? ____%

A Look at the picture. Complete the sentences. Use *should* or *shouldn't*.

1. Li ___should___ stay home.

2. She _____ drink tea.

3. She _____ go to work today.

4. She _____ take some medicine.

5. She _____ visit her friends.

6. She _____ rest in bed.

B Linda's neighborhood isn't safe. Write sentences about Linda. Use the words in parentheses and *should* or *shouldn't*. What should Linda do? What shouldn't she do?

1. (lock the door)

    _She should lock the door._____

2. (walk alone at night)

    _____

3. (say hello to her neighbors)

    _____

4. (open the door to strangers)

    _____

5. (leave the building door open)

    _____

C Complete the questions.

1. **A:** Where _should I go?_____

    B: You should go home.

2. **A:** What _____

    B: You should drink hot tea.

3. **A:** When _____

    B: You should call the doctor tomorrow morning.

4. **A:** When _____

    B: You should come back to work on Friday.

D Complete the sentences. Use *should* or *shouldn't* and the verbs in the box.

| drive | stop | talk | wear | ~~slow down~~ |

1. The driver ___should slow down___ near the school.

2. He _____ at the traffic light.

3. He _____ his seatbelt.

4. He _____ on his cell phone.

5. He _____ 80 mph.

E Complete the conversation. Use *should* or *shouldn't* and the verbs in parentheses.

Olivia: Hi, I'm Olivia. I'm a new student in this class. Our teacher, Mr. Lewis, wants me to learn the classroom rules. Can you help me?

Dan: Hi, Olivia. It's nice to meet you. Well, one important rule in this class is to be on time. You ___shouldn't be late___ (be late) to class.

1

Sara: Hi, Olivia. I'm Sara. You _____ (speak) English at home,

2
and you _____ (sleep) in class.

3

Dan: Oh, and you _____ (do) your homework, and you

4
_____ (forget) your books.

5

Sara: And one more rule. You _____ (have fun)!

6

Olivia: OK, thanks for your help!

F **Grammar Boost** Complete the sentences. Use *should* or *have to*.

1. You can't park in front of the school. You _____have to_____ park in the parking lot.

2. I think you _____ listen to the radio. It helps you learn English.

3. Where is your hard hat? You _____ wear a hard hat in this work area. It's the rule.

4. Don't forget! You _____ pay the electric bill today. It's very important!

5. I think you _____ get more exercise. It's good for you.

> **Need help?**
>
> **should vs. have to**
> should = It's a good idea.
> have to = It's necessary.

LESSON 4 | Everyday conversation

A Complete the conversation. Use the words in the box.

a car accident	anyone hurt	the address
~~Emergency~~	ambulance	should I do

A: 911. _____ Emergency _____.
₁

B: Help! There was _____ across the street from my house!
₂

A: OK. What's _____?
₃

B: It's 932 Eastside Drive.

A: Is _____?
₄

B: I don't know. I can't see them. I think so. The people can't get out of the car.

A: OK. Help is on the way.

B: What _____?
₅

A: Nothing. Stay there. Wait for the _____ and fire trucks.
₆

B Match the questions with the answers.

_d_ 1. Who needs help?   a. 54 Highland Avenue.

____ 2. What's the emergency?   b. Yes, you should.

____ 3. Where's the emergency? c. Someone's choking.

____ 4. Should I call 911?   d. A woman.

C Look at the picture. You're talking to a 911 operator. Answer the questions.

1. What's the emergency?

   <u>There's a car accident.</u>

2. Where's the emergency?

   _____

3. Who needs help?

   _____

4. Should Sonya wait for help?

   _____

A Read the article.

SAFETY ⊕ FIRST

Every month at *Parents and Kids* magazine, we give you safety information. We want your children to be safe.
This month, we are giving you information on bicycle safety. Here are some ways to protect your children:

- Your children should wear bicycle helmets.

- They should not ride their bicycles at night.

- In the daytime, they should wear clothing with colors like red and yellow. This helps other people see them.

- Do you ride a bicycle? You should wear a helmet and colorful clothing. Your children see you as an example.

Every month we ask you some safety questions on the Internet. Here are our questions and your answers:

Do your children wear bicycle helmets?

64% Yes   36% No

Do you wear a bicycle helmet?

12% Yes   88% No

helmet

B Look at the article in A. Mark the sentences T (true) or F (false.)

__T__ 1. This month, the magazine is about bicycle safety.

_____ 2. Bicycle helmets don't protect children.

_____ 3. In the daytime, children should wear colors like red or yellow.

_____ 4. Parents should wear bicycle helmets, too.

_____ 5. Thirty-five percent of children wear bicycle helmets.

_____ 6. Parents always wear helmets.

A Complete the puzzle.

Missing Letters and Secret Message

1. s a f e t y b o o t s

2. _ _ _

3. _ _ _ _ _ _ _ _ _ _ _

4. _ _ _ _ _ _ _

5. _ _ _ _ _ _ _

6. _ _ _ _ _ _ _

7. _ _ _ _ _ _ _ _ _ _

8. _ _ _ _ _ _ _

9. _ _ _ _ _ _ _ _

B Look at the letters in the boxes. What's the secret message?

$\underset{1}{\text{B}}$ $\underset{2}{\rule{1em}{0.4pt}}$ $\underset{3}{\rule{1em}{0.4pt}}$ $\underset{4}{\rule{1em}{0.4pt}}$ $\underset{5}{\rule{1em}{0.4pt}}$ $\underset{6}{\rule{1em}{0.4pt}}$ $\underset{7}{\rule{1em}{0.4pt}}$ $\underset{8}{\rule{1em}{0.4pt}}$ $\underset{9}{\rule{1em}{0.4pt}}$!

UNIT 12

Free Time

LESSON 1 — Vocabulary

A Look at the weather map. Complete the sentences. Use the words in the box.

| cloudy | cold | hot | raining | snowing | sunny |

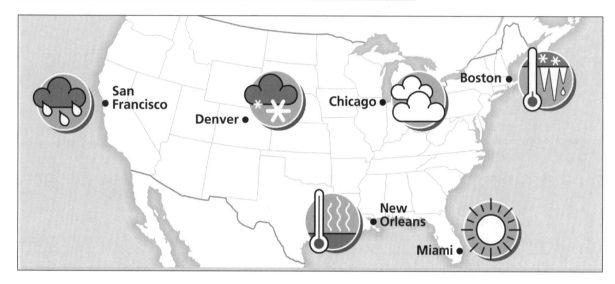

1. In Boston, it's _____cold_____.

2. In Miami, it's _____.

3. Today, it's _____ in New Orleans.

4. In Chicago, it's _____.

5. It's _____ in Denver.

6. It's _____ in San Francisco.

B Cross out (X) the words that do NOT belong.

1.	fall	cloudy	summer	winter
2.	go to the beach	spring	have a picnic	go out to eat
3.	summer	fall	spring	sunny
4.	Father's Day	Independence Day	September	Thanksgiving
5.	go to the movies	go swimming	stay home	cloudy

LESSON 2 Life stories

A Complete the sentences. Use the words in the box.

have to work	can't wait	a lot of fun	This Saturday
~~for the weekend~~	watch a soccer	have a picnic	

Ken can't wait _____for the weekend_____.
                            1

He doesn't _____
                            2
on Saturday or Sunday. Ken has

_____ with his friends
                3
and coworkers. _____,
                                    4

they're going to _____ game and _____ in
                            5   6

the park. Ken _____ for Saturday!
                            7

B Read the bus schedule and the paragraph.

Stanville Municipal Bus Co. Weekend Schedule				
Hill Street Terminal	**Memorial Hospital**	**Pine Street Park**	**North Street School**	**Stanville Shopping Mall**
Leave 8:30 a.m.	8:40	8:55	9:05	9:15
Leave 10:30 a.m.	10:40	10:55	11:05	11:15
Leave 12:30 p.m.	12:40	12:55	1:05	1:15
Leave 2:30 p.m.	2:40	2:55	3:05	3:15
Leave 3:30 p.m.	3:40	3:55	4:05	4:15

Ken gets the bus at the Hill Street Terminal. He is meeting his friend at Pine Street Park at 11:00. Ken and his friend want to see a movie at the Stanville Shopping Mall. The movie starts at 4:00.

C Look at the schedule and paragraph in B. Answer the questions.

1. What time should he take the bus at the Hill Street Terminal? _____10:30_____

2. What time does the bus stop at the park? _____

3. What time should they take the bus at Pine Street Park? _____2:55_____

4. What time does the bus stop at the Stanville Shopping Mall? _____

A **Unscramble the sentences.**

1. play / Ken / going to / baseball / is

   <u>Ken is going to play baseball.</u>

2. picnic / going to / have / We / a / are

   _____

3. am / going to / stay / I / home

   _____

4. movie / a / watch / Rita and Paul / are / going to

   _____

5. are / to / beach / You / going to / go / the

   _____

6. Isabel / jogging / going to / go / is

   _____

B **Complete the questions. Use _What, Who, When,_ or _Where_. Then match the questions with the answers.**

<u>c</u> 1. <u>What</u> are Karen and Marie going to do tonight?

_____ 2. _____ is Hector going to study?

_____ 3. _____ are Mr. and Mrs. Smith going to eat dinner with?

_____ 4. _____ is Yoshi going to go after class?

a. He's going to study on Wednesday.

b. They're going to eat dinner with their children.

c. They're going to go jogging.

d. He's going to go to the gym.

C Write the questions. Use the future with *be going to* and *What* or *When*.

1. **A:** <u>When are you going to go to the beach?</u>

   B: I'm going to go to the beach <u>on Saturday</u>.

2. **A:** _____

   B: I'm going to <u>go swimming</u>.

3. **A:** _____

   B: Lucas is going to <u>visit some friends</u>.

4. **A:** _____

   B: We're going to study in the park <u>tomorrow</u>.

D Complete the sentences. Use the future with *be going to*.

1. I <u>work</u> on the weekend. <u>I'm going to work</u> _____ this Sunday.

2. We usually <u>play</u> tennis in the park, but tomorrow

   _____ at school.

3. Maria often <u>exercises</u> with me in the evening. Tomorrow

   _____ with me in the afternoon.

4. My friends usually <u>watch</u> a baseball game on Saturday, but

   _____ a football game this Saturday.

5. You always <u>study</u> on the weekend. _____ this
   weekend, too.

E 🚀 Grammar Boost   What about you? Complete the sentences.
    Use your own ideas.

Tonight, I'm going to clean the house and watch a movie.

1. Tonight, I'm going to _____

2. Tomorrow, _____

3. On Saturday, _____

4. Next year, _____

A   Unscramble the sentences. Complete the conversation.

A: (going to / tonight / What / are / we / do)

What are we going to do tonight?
1

B: (see / Do / a / you / movie / want / to)

_____
2

A: (playing / _The Long Trail Home_ / is / 6:30 / at)

_____
3

B: (the / tickets / much / How / are)

_____
4

A: ($8.00 / for / They / adults / are)

_____
5

B: (bargain / a / That's / great)

_____
6

B   [Real-life math]   **Read the movie ad. Answer the questions. Use complete sentences.**

1. Kate is going to see _The Long Trail Home_ at 6:30. What time does the movie finish?

   It finishes at 8:30.

2. Can she take the bus home at 8:15?

   _____

3. Kate's friends, Mike and Alice, are going to see the movie at 4:00. How much are their tickets going to be?

   _____

4. What time are Mike and Alice going to leave the movie theater?

   _____

5. There are three adults and two children buying tickets for the 6:30 movie. How much are their tickets going to be?

   _____

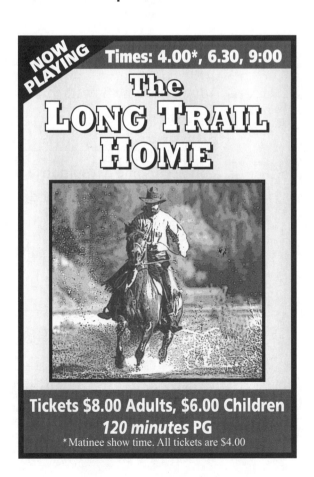

NOW PLAYING   Times: 4.00*, 6.30, 9:00

The LONG TRAIL HOME

Tickets $8.00 Adults, $6.00 Children
120 minutes PG
*Matinee show time. All tickets are $4.00

A Match the pictures with the holiday messages.

_b_ 1.

a. Happy Mother's Day

____ 2.

b. Happy Father's Day

____ 3.

c. Happy Birthday

____ 4.

d. Happy Valentine's Day

B Look at the phone book. Answer the questions. Use complete sentences.

1. You want some flowers for a party. Where do you call?

   You call Flowers for You.

2. You need some decorations for a New Year's Party. What number do you call?

   _____

3. You need food for a large party. What number do you call?

   _____

4. When does the Party Store close?

   _____

5. Where can you find the Party Store on the Internet?

   _____

472 PARTY STORES

PARTY TIME

Have a party today!

· Decorations
· Balloons
· Gift Cards

Open every day 9-5
website: www.partystore.net

31 Washington Ave
555-3434

Flowers For You 555-2300
Food for Your Party Catering 555-6899

A **Find the words in the puzzle. Use the words in the box.**

snowing	~~Independence Day~~	winter	New Year's Day
raining	Valentine's Day	birthday	Thanksgiving
sunny	summer	spring	fall
hot	cold	holiday	cloudy

```
W  B  K  A  N  T  E  R  F  A  L  L  O  R  A
I  I  O  N  E  W  Y  E  A  R  S  D  A  Y  V
N  R  T  H  A  N  K  S  G  I  V  I  N  G  A
T  T  Y  S  N  W  T  I  O  P  L  L  I  C  L
E  H  S  U  N  N  Y  N  H  O  T  A  R  L  E
R  D  U  M  T  A  P  E  A  U  I  W  T  O  N
U  A  O  M  I  L  C  O  H  C  D  F  H  U  T
M  Y  R  E  F  M  E  K  L  O  Y  A  D  D  I
O  S  P  R  I  N  G  H  O  L  I  D  A  Y  N
P  E  E  O  Z  A  I  M  W  D  R  D  Y  Q  E
R  A  I  N  I  N  G  T  E  N  A  A  U  P  S
N  H  S  N  O  W  I  N  G  R  T  C  O  M  D
L  O  X  U  V  A  L  F  T  T  L  N  K  S  A
I  N  D  E  P  E  N  D  E  N  C  E  D  A  Y
```

B **Look at the words in A. Write 4 seasons, 6 weather words, and 6 holidays and special occasions.**

Unit 1 In the Classroom

Lesson 1 Vocabulary
page 2

A
say – 3
open – 2
point to – 5
close – 4
sit down – 6
repeat – 7
stand up – 8
B
Answers will vary.

Lesson 2 Life stories
page 3

B
2. a
3. a
4. a
5. b
6. b
C
Answers will vary.

Lesson 3 Grammar
page 4

A
2. are
3. am
4. are
5. are
6. is
7. is
8. is
B
2. are
3. are
4. are
5. am
6. is
7. is
8. are
C
2. We are not in the classroom.
3. You are not a teacher.
4. They are not in my group.
5. I am not at my desk.
6. It is not my dictionary.
7. She is not a student.
8. Elena and Dan are not teachers.

page 5

D
2. We aren't teachers.
3. The teacher isn't here.
4. She isn't in the classroom.
5. You're my partner.
6. They're listening.
7. I'm not at school.
8. He's a teacher.
E
2. They are not students.
3. You are my classmate.
4. We are in school.
5. It is my book.
6. She is not my teacher.

Lesson 4 Everyday conversation
page 6

A
2. How are
3. And you
4. Fine
5. you later
B
Answers will vary.

Lesson 5 Real-life reading
page 7

A
2. ask for help
3. go to school
4. listen to the radio
B
2. a
3. c
4. b
C
Answers will vary.

Another look
page 8

A
2. How are you
3. Tell me your address
4. What's your phone number
5. Sign your name
B
Answers will vary.

Unit 2 My Classmates

Lesson 1 Vocabulary
page 9

A
2. 9:30, nine thirty
3. 10:15, ten fifteen
4. 3:45, three forty-five
5. 1:30, one thirty
6. 8:15, eight fifteen
B
Time: 4:30, 2:00
Day: Friday, Thursday
Month: March, October, January
Date: 11/20/88, 3/16/05, 7/18/07

Lesson 2 Life stories
page 10

B
2. El Salvador
3. date
4. telephone
5. live
6. address
C
Answers will vary.

Lesson 3 Grammar
page 11

A
2. proud
3. angry
4. happy
5. hungry
6. tired
B
2. d
3. e
4. a
5. b
C
2. Is Lilia proud?
3. Are Carol and Pam from Vietnam?
4. Is Daniel tired?
5. Are you hungry?

page 12

D
2. Are the students tired?
3. Is Juan from Mexico?

4. Is the teacher in the classroom?
5. Is this workbook yellow?
6. Are we studying?
E
2. a – Where are you from?
3. d – What is your date of birth?
4. b – Where is Luc?

Lesson 4 Everyday conversation
page 13

B
2. My first name is Yoshi.
3. I'm married.
4. My address is 3933 Ross Avenue, San Jose, CA 95124.
5. My date of birth is 5/6/76.
6. I'm from Japan.
C
Answers will vary.

Lesson 5 Real-life reading
page 14

A
2. countries
3. population
C
2. a
3. a
4. b

Another look
page 15

A
Months: ~~Sunday~~
Dates: ~~12.10~~
Times: ~~1990~~
Colors: ~~month~~
Feelings: ~~today~~
Countries: ~~April~~
Continents: ~~Avenue~~
B
Answers will vary.

Unit 3 Family and Friends

Lesson 1 Vocabulary
page 16

A
Answers will vary.
B
2. Al
3. father
4. Amy, grandparents

Lesson 2 Life stories
page 17

A
2. My
3. eyes
4. hair
5. is
6. Pavel *or* Pavel Turek
7. are
8. blue
9. My
10. hair
B
Answers will vary.

Lesson 3 Grammar
page 18

A
2. His
3. Our
4. Her
5. Their
6. your
B
2. f
3. e
4. a
5. b
6. c
C
2. Her
3. Her
4. their
5. our
6. your
7. Its
8. your

page 19

D
2. His eyes are blue.
3. His hair is black.
4. Her name is Sasha Tomlin.
5. Her eyes are green.
6. Her hair is blond.
E
2. A: Paul's B: His
3. A: Sasha's B: Her
4. A: Sasha's B: Her
5. A: Paul's B: His
6. A: Sasha's B: Her
7. A: Sasha's B: Her
8. A: Paul's B: His

Lesson 4 Everyday conversation
page 20

A
2. It's Tuesday
3. the date today
4. October 10th
5. that's right
6. birthday
B
2. June 21st
3. February 22nd
4. August 9th
5. November 20th
6. July 31st
C
2. The date is June 5th.
3. Marie's birthday is June 8th.
4. June 9th is Tuesday.

Lesson 5 Real-life reading
page 21

B
2. a
3. b
4. b

Another look
page 22

A
Days:
2. Friday
3. Thursday
4. Tuesday
5. Wednesday
Months:
1. August
2. January
3. September
4. October
5. November
B
2. Sue's hair is black.
3. Her eyes are green.
4. My aunt is tall and beautiful.
5. Our uncle has blue eyes.
6. Your cousin's hair is brown.

Unit 4 At Home

Lesson 1 Vocabulary
page 23

A
bed – 3
table – 10
sink – 2
sofa – 8
dresser – 4

refrigerator – 9
stove – 11
chair – 6
TV – 5
rug – 7

B
2. The stove is in the kitchen.
3. No, it isn't.
4. No, it isn't.

Lesson 2 Life stories
page 24

A
2. yard
3. the kitchen
4. cooking dinner
5. bedroom
6. playing games
7. living room
8. washing the car

B
This/These
2. This
3. These
That/Those
1. That
2. That
3. Those

Lesson 3 Grammar
page 25

A
2. She
3. We
4. You
5. They
6. I

B
2. is doing
3. am reading
4. are eating
5. is sleeping
6. is listening

C
2. My brother is mopping the kitchen.
3. Our friends are washing the car.
4. My mother is vacuuming the rug.
5. Our cousin is dusting the bookcase.
6. I am watching TV.

page 26

D
2. What are Patty and Rose doing? They're listening to the radio.
3. What are David and Maritza doing? They're playing games.
4. What is Pete doing? He's washing the car.

E
2. mopping
3. doing
4. giving
5. closing
6. stopping

Lesson 4 Everyday conversation
page 27

B
2. paying
3. I help you
4. the electric bill
5. the due date
6. May 12th

C
2. They are looking at it.
3. We are calling him.
4. I'm giving them to her.
5. She is listening to it.
6. It is sending the bill to us.

Lesson 5 Real-life reading
page 28

B
2. √
3. √
4. X
5. √
6. X

Another look
page 29

A
2. cleaning
3. stove
4. electric
5. mopping
6. bedroom
7. phone
8. eating
9. paying

B
1. b i l l (s)
2.   c l e (a) n i n g
3.   s t o (v) e
4.   e l (e) c t r i c
5.   (m) o p p i n g
6. b e d r (o) o m
7.   p h o (n) e
8.   (e) a t i n g
9.   p a (y) i n g

C
Save money

Lesson 1 Vocabulary
page 30

A
supermarket – 8
fire station – 2
restaurant – 7
bicycle – 10
gas station – 5
bus stop – 9
pharmacy – 6
bank – 3
parking lot – 4

B
2. The fire station is on Post Road.
3. The supermarket is on Center Street.
4. The school is on Post Road.

Lesson 2 Life stories
page 31

A
2. c
3. a
4. d

B
2. an apartment
3. my neighborhood
4. across from my
5. next to the
6. a bank

Lesson 3 Grammar
page 32

A
2. There are
3. There is
4. There are
5. There are
6. There is
7. There is
8. There are

B
2. There is a movie theater across from my home.
3. There are some restaurants next to the school.
4. There is a parking lot behind the school.
5. There is an apartment building between the school and the park.
6. There is a bus stop in front of the movie theater.

7. There is a supermarket next to the park.
8. There is a hospital behind the supermarket.

page 33

C
2. A: Is there
   B: Yes, there is.
3. A: Is there
   B: No, there isn't.
4. A: Are there
   B: No, there aren't.
5. A: Are there
   B: Yes, there are.
6. A: Is there
   B: Yes, there is.
D
2. A: Is there
   B: Answers will vary.
3. A: Are there
   B: Answers will vary.
4. A: Are there
   B: Answers will vary.

Lesson 4 Everyday conversation
page 34

A
2. there
3. straight
4. left
5. blocks
6. turn
7. right
8. between
B
2. 347
3. 44
4. 498

Lesson 5 Real-life reading
page 35

A
Answers will vary.
C
2. a
3. a
4. b
5. b
6. a

Another look
page 36

A
ACROSS
4. bus
7. There

8. fire
10. station
11. clinic
DOWN
1. between
3. across
5. school
6. office
9. bank
B

Unit 6 Daily Routines

Lesson 1 Vocabulary
page 37

A
Answers will vary.
B
Answers will vary.
C
Answers will vary.

Lesson 2 Life stories
page 38

B
2. Sunday
3. 4:00 p.m.
4. vacuum the rugs
5. mop the floors
6. eat dinner
7. wash the tables, the manager
8. 12:00 a.m. *or* midnight
C
Answers will vary.

Lesson 3 Grammar
page 39

A
2. watches
3. studies
4. takes
5. plays
6. exercises
C
2. She works on the weekends.
3. She rides the bus in the morning.

4. She visits Judy after work.

page 40

D
2. does; She does housework from 8 a.m. to 4 p.m.
3. do; They exercise from 4 p.m. to 6 p.m.
4. do; They eat dinner from 6 p.m. to 7 p.m.
5. does; He does housework from 8 p.m. to 10 p.m.
6. does; She works from 8 p.m. to 2 a.m.
E
2. e, Do
3. a, Are
4. b, Is
5. f, Are
6. d, Do

Lesson 4 Everyday conversation
page 41

A
2. a
3. b
4. c
B
2. help me
3. fill the
4. the paper here
5. problem
6. my job
C
2. plays
3. fixes
4. watches
5. works
6. exercises

Lesson 5 Real-life reading
page 42

B
2. b
3. a
4. a
5. b
C
Answers will vary.

Another look
page 43

A
2. come
3. wash
4. get
5. drink

6. study
7. help
8. make

B

1.		a	n	s	w	e	r
2.				c	o	m	e
3.	w	a	s	h			
4.				g	e	t	
5.				d	r	i	n	k
6.		s	t	u	d	y	
7.			h	e	l	p	
8.	m	a	k	e			

C
schedule

Unit 7 Shop and Spend

Lesson 1 Vocabulary
page 44

A
25¢ – 4
1¢ – 5
$5.00 – 6
$1.00 – 3
10¢ – 2
75¢ – 8
50¢ – 7

B
2. It's $12.00.
3. They're $34.00.
4. It's $75.00.
5. It's $45.00.
6. They're $2.25.
7. They're $17.50.
8. It's $25.00.

Lesson 2 Life stories
page 45

B
2. A
3. A
4. A
5. B
6. B

C
2. She wears a uniform and a hat.
3. She wears a blouse and a skirt.

Lesson 3 Grammar
page 46

A
2. f
3. e
4. a
5. b
6. d

B
2. A: Does B: she doesn't
3. A: Does B: he doesn't
4. A: Does B: he does
5. A: Do B: they do
6. A: Do B: I do

page 47

C
2. want
3. need
4. has
5. wants
6. needs

D
2. Does John want a new house?
3. Does Sara want the blue blouse?
4. Do you want the green sweater?

E
2. A: Do B: have
3. A: Do B: have
4. A: Does B: have

Lesson 4 Everyday conversation
page 48

A
2. How much
3. on sale
4. What size
5. Here's
6. take it

B
2. It's $16.95.
3. The customer wants two sweaters.
4. They're $12.95.
5. It's a large. *or* It's large.

C
Receipt #2: change is $2.77
Receipt #3: change is $14.13

Lesson 5 Real-life reading
page 49

B
2. PAY TO THE ORDER OF
3. numbers
4. SIGNATURE

C
DATE: answers will vary
PAY TO THE ORDER OF: Super Store
DOLLAR box: 32.45
AMOUNT: thirty-two dollars and forty-five cents
MEMO: radio
SIGNATURE: answers will vary

Another look
page 50

A
2. T
3. S
4. O
5. N
6. S
7. A
8. L
9. E

B
It's on sale

Unit 8 Eating Well

Lesson 1 Vocabulary
page 51

A
2. basket
3. bagger
4. aisle
5. checker

B
bananas – 6
tomatoes – 8
milk – 9
eggs – 3
potatoes – 5
apples – 4
onions – 2
lettuce – 7

C
2. a
3. b
4. b

Lesson 2 Life stories
page 52

A
2. a customer
3. a shopping list
4. is buying
5. once a week
6. good prices

B
Picture #1: potatoes, eggs, fish
Picture #2: milk, bread, chicken, soup
Picture #3: bananas, grapes, cookies, ice cream

Lesson 3 Grammar
page 53

B
2. every day

3. twice a week
4. never
C
2. I never eat ice cream.
3. Paula eats pizza once a week.
4. They have dinner with friends four times a month.
D
Answers will vary.

page 54

E
Answers will vary.
F
Answers will vary.
G
Possible answers:
1. I always / often / sometimes / never study English in the evening.
2. I always / often / sometimes / never ride the bus.
3. I always /often / sometimes / never get up at 7 a.m.
4. I always / often / sometimes / never go to bed at 8 p.m.

Lesson 4 Everyday conversation
page 55

A
2. I'd like
3. please
4. anything to drink
5. I do
6. coffee too
7. That's one
8. right
B
1 vegetable soup $3.95
1 salad $4.95
2 cups of coffee $3.00
Total: $18.85

Lesson 5 Real-life reading
page 56

B
2. a
3. b
4. a
5. b

Another look
page 57

2. tea; coffee
3. pizza; soup, salad
4. chicken, salad; fish, potato
5. large; small

Unit 9 Your Health
Lesson 1 Vocabulary
page 58

A
2. head
3. mouth
4. neck
5. chest
6. arm
7. leg
8. hand
9. foot
B
2. earache
3. fever
4. doctor
5. receptionist
6. nurse

Lesson 2 Life stories
page 59

A
2. sore throat
3. to the doctor
4. examines her
5. her temperature
6. a prescription
7. goes home
8. the medicine
9. drinks some
B
Answers will vary.

Lesson 3 Grammar
page 60

A
2. has
3. have
4. have
5. have
6. has
B
2. has to, has
3. has, has to
4. have to, have
5. have, have to
C
2. A: Why does he have to take medicine? B: has
3. A: Why do they have to go to the store? B: have to
4. A: Why does she have to run every day? B: has to
5. A: Why do you have to leave early? B: have to

page 61

D
2. does he have to buy?
3. do they have to go tomorrow?
4. do I have to go to bed?
5. does she have to take the pills?
E
2. You have got a nice family.
3. The teacher has got to leave early tonight.
4. They have got to work this weekend.
5. I have got to stay home. I have got a fever.
6. You have got to exercise more.

Lesson 4 Everyday conversation
page 62

A
2. Monday
3. 11 a.m.
4. May 23rd
B
2. has an opening
3. that okay
4. it is
5. Tuesday, October 5th
6. 9 a.m.
C
Patient: Karen Hill
Has an appointment on:
Tuesday, October 5th
At: 9 a.m.
With: Dr. Durgin

Lesson 5 Real-life reading
page 63

B
2. F
3. T
4. F
5. F
C
2. twice a day
3. yes
4. one

Another look
page 64

A
2. Take two pills a day.
3. Rest in bed.
4. Take one pill twice a day.
5. Do not take this with alcohol.
6. Exercise every day.

7. Call the doctor.
8. Eat healthy food.
B
Answers will vary.

Unit 10 Getting the Job

Lesson 1 Vocabulary
page 65

A
2. janitor
3. childcare worker
4. cook
5. delivery person
6. plumber
B
1. garden
2. pharmacist, pharmacy

Lesson 2 Life stories
page 66

A
2. part-time
3. in the evenings
4. childcare worker
5. at Children's Castle
6. a full-time job
B
2. Internet
3. help-wanted ads
4. full-time
5. as a bus driver
6. in person
7. completes a form
8. interview for the job

Lesson 3 Grammar
page 67

A
2. was
3. was
4. were not
5. was
6. was
7. were not
8. were
B
2. A: Were B: No, they weren't.
3. A: Were B: No, they weren't.
4. A: Was B: No, she wasn't.
5. A: Was B: No, he wasn't.
6. A: Were B: Yes, they were.

page 68

C
2. They were students from 1995 to 2001.

3. Min was a nurse from 2001 to 2003.
4. Hung-ju was not a teacher in Korea.
5. Min and Hung-ju were in San Francisco last year.
6. Min was not in Korea last year.
D
2. A: Was B: Yes, she was.
3. A: Was B: No, she wasn't.
4. A: Is B: No, she isn't.
5. A: Does B: Yes, she does.

Lesson 4 Everyday conversation
page 69

A
2. work experience
3. I do
4. an office manager
5. I can use
6. weekends
7. I can
8. You're hired
B
Job Titles and Number of Years: office manager, 6 years; office worker, 1 year; Skills: use a computer, make copies

Lesson 5 Real-life reading
page 70

B
2. F
3. T
4. F
5. T
6. T
7. T
8. T

Another look
page 71

A
2. garage
3. server
4. restaurant
5. gardens
6. gardener
7. school
8. janitor
B
Jobs: janitor, gardener, server, cook, manager
Workplaces: garage, school, garden, restaurant, kitchen, office

C
2. A janitor works in a school and cleans the building *or* cleans buildings.
3. A gardener works in a garden and plants flowers.
4. A server works in a restaurant and serves food.
5. A cook works in a kitchen and cooks food.
6. A manager works in an office and manages a business.

Unit 11 Safety First

Lesson 1 Vocabulary
page 72

A
2. road work
3. school crossing
4. no left turn
5. speed limit
6. stop
B
2. ~~safety glasses~~
3. ~~safe~~
4. ~~factory worker~~
C
2. careless
3. dangerous
4. emergency exit

Lesson 2 Life stories
page 73

A
1. X
2. √
3. X
4. √
5. √
6. √
B
2. going fast
3. slow down
4. check the speed
5. careful
C
2. 85%

Lesson 3 Grammar
page 74

A
2. should
3. shouldn't
4. should
5. shouldn't
6. should

B

2. She shouldn't walk alone at night.
3. She should say hello to her neighbors.
4. She shouldn't open the door to strangers.
5. She shouldn't leave the building door open.

C

2. should I do?
3. should I call the doctor?
4. should I come back to work?

page 75

D

2. should stop
3. should wear
4. shouldn't talk
5. shouldn't drive

E

2. should speak
3. shouldn't sleep
4. should do
5. shouldn't forget
6. should have fun

F

2. should
3. have to
4. have to
5. should

Lesson 4 Everyday conversation
page 76

A

2. a car accident
3. the address
4. anyone hurt
5. should I do
6. ambulance

B

2. c
3. a
4. b

C

2. It's on the corner of Lincoln Street and Main Street.
3. Sonya needs help.
4. Yes, she should wait for help.

Lesson 5 Real-life reading
page 77

B

2. F
3. T
4. T

5. F
6. F

Another look
page 78

A

1. safety boots
2. fire
3. school crossing
4. hard hat
5. road work
6. seatbelt
7. safety gloves
8. ambulance
9. speed limit

B

Be careful

Unit 12 Free Time

Lesson 1 Vocabulary
page 79

A

2. sunny
3. hot
4. cloudy
5. snowing
6. raining

B

2. ~~spring~~
3. ~~sunny~~
4. ~~September~~
5. ~~cloudy~~

Lesson 2 Life stories
page 80

A

2. have to work
3. a lot of fun
4. This Saturday
5. watch a soccer
6. have a picnic
7. can't wait

C

2. 10:55
4. 3:15

Lesson 3 Grammar
page 81

A

2. We are going to have a picnic.
3. I am going to stay home.
4. Paul and Rita *or* Rita and Paul are going to watch a movie.

5. You are going to go to the beach.
6. Isabel is going to go jogging.

B

2. When, a
3. Who, b
4. Where, d

page 82

C

2. A: What are you going to do?
3. A: What is Lucas going to do?
4. A: When are you going to study in the park?

D

2. we're going to play
3. she's going to exercise
4. they're going to watch
5. You're going to study

E

Answers will vary.

Lesson 4 Everyday conversation
page 83

A

2. Do you want to see a movie?
3. *The Long Trail Home* is playing at 6:30.
4. How much are the tickets?
5. They are $8.00 for adults.
6. That's a great bargain.

B

2. No, she can't.
3. Their tickets are going to be $8 *or* $4.00 each.
4. They're going to leave at 6:00.
5. Their tickets are going to be $36.00.

Lesson 5 Real-life reading
page 84

A

2. c
3. d
4. a

B

2. You call 555-3434.
3. You call 555-6899.
4. The Party Store closes at 5:00.
5. You can find the Party Store on the Internet at www.partystore.net.

Another look
page 85

A

B

Seasons: winter, summer,

```
W  B  K  A  N  T  E  R  F  A  L  L  O  R  A
I  I  O  N  E  W  Y  E  A  R  S  D  A  Y  V
N  R  T  H  A  N  K  S  G  I  V  I  N  G  A
T  Y  S  N  W  T  I  O  P  L  L  I  C  L
E  H  S  U  N  N  Y  N  H  O  T  A  R  L  E
R  D  U  M  T  A  P  E  A  U  I  W  T  O  N
U  A  O  M  I  L  C  O  H  C  D  F  H  U  T
M  Y  R  E  F  M  E  K  L  O  Y  A  D  D  I
O  S  P  R  I  N  G  H  O  L  I  D  A  Y  N
P  E  E  O  Z  A  I  M  W  D  R  D  Y  Q  E
R  A  I  N  I  N  G  T  E  N  A  A  U  P  S
N  H  S  N  O  W  I  N  G  R  T  C  O  M  D
L  O  X  U  V  A  L  F  T  T  L  N  K  S  A
I  N  D  E  P  E  N  D  E  N  C  E  D  A  Y
```

spring, fall
Weather: hot, cold, raining,
snowing, cloudy, sunny
Holidays and special occasions:
birthday, New Year's Day,
Thanksgiving, Valentine's Day,
holiday, Independence Day